ABOUT THE AUTHOR

Mustapha Matura was born in Trinidad and moved to England in 1960. His first full-length stage play was AS TIME GOES BY, produced at the Traverse Theatre, Edinburgh, and the Royal Court, London, which won both the George Devine and John Whiting awards in 1971.

His many stage plays include: BLACK PIECES (1970); BAKERLOO LINE (1972); NICE (1973); PLAY MAS (1974), which won the *London Evening Standard*'s Most Promising Playwright Award and transferred to the West End; BLACK SLAVES WHITE CHAINS (1975); RUM 'N COCA COLA (1976); BREAD (1976); ANOTHER TUESDAY (1978); MORE MORE (1978); INDEPENDENCE (1979); WELCOME HOME JACKO (1979); A DYING BUSINESS (1980); ONE RULE (1981); MEETINGS (1982); PLAYBOY OF THE WEST INDIES (1984); and TRINIDAD SISTERS (1988).

Several of his stage plays have been seen in America, including: RUM 'N COCA COLA (Brooklyn Academy, New York 1976); NICE (Arena Stage, Washington D.C. 1980); PLAY MAS (Goodman Theatre, Chicago 1981); and MEETINGS (Phoenix APA, New York 1981).

He also writes for television, including the highly acclaimed and popular series, NO PROBLEM.

To Ingrid Cayal, Maya, Dominic, and Ann

PLAYBOY OF THE WEST INDIES was originally commissioned and produced by the Oxford Playhouse Company, Oxford, England. The play opened on January 17, 1984, and the production toured nationally, ending in a run at London's Tricycle Theatre with the following cast, in order of appearance:

PEGGY . . . . .Joan Ann Maynard
STANLEY . . . . Jason Rose
PHIL . . . . .Tommy Eytle
JIMMY . . . . Frank Singuineau
MIKEY . . . . Rudolph Walker
KEN . . . . Jim Findley
MAMA BENIN . . . . Mona Hammond
ALICE . . . . Joy Richardson
IVY . . . . .Jackie De Peza
MAC . . . . .T-Bone Wilson

Director . . . . Nicolas Kent

The play was remounted for further performances at the Tricycle Theatre in April of that year with the following cast changes:

STANLEY . . . . .Stefan Kalipha
PHIL . . . . .Ruddy L. Davis
MAC . . . . Ram John Holder

PLAYBOY OF THE WEST INDIES had its American premiere at the Court Theatre in Chicago on April 21, 1988, with Nicholas Rudall, Artistic Director, and Mark Tiarks, Producing Director. The cast was, in order of appearance:

PEGGY . . . . .Celeste Williams
STANLEY . . . . Stefan Kalipha
PHIL . . . . Ivory Ocean
JIMMY . . . . .Chuck Smith
MIKEY . . . . Ernest Perry, Jr.
KEN . . . . .Don Franklin
MAMA BENIN . . . . .Pat Bowie
ALICE . . . . Cherene Snow
IVY . . . . Crystal Walker
MAC . . . . .John Cothran, Jr.

Director . . . . Nicolas Kent
Set design . . . . Adrianne Lobel
Lighting . . . . Michael Rourke
Costumes . . . . .Jeff Bauer
Production stage manager . . . . Cathryn Bulicek

CHARACTERS

(In order of appearance)

PEGGY
STANLEY
PHIL
JIMMY
MIKEY
KEN
MAMA BENIN
ALICE
IVY
MAC

J. M. Synge's PLAYBOY OF THE WESTERN WORLD was first produced on January 26, 1912, in Dublin, Ireland. The play was set in Mayo. Mustapha Matura's version is set in Mayaro, Trinidad, in August 1950.

ACT ONE

9:30 pm on Friday

ACT TWO

9:30 am on Saturday

ACT THREE

5:00 pm on the same day

There is an intermission between each act; the setting remains the same.

GLOSSARY

ACT ONE

SAPATS: a cheap type of footwear
OBEAH WOMAN: a woman who practices folk religion
PICONG: a type of teasing
MANZANILLA: a beach next to Mayaro
FIRE ONE: drink one (rum or spirits)
PACKOTI HOUSE: a brothel
BASIL DE BOOBALEE: a form of dummy (like a Guy
Fawkes or a scarecrow)
GARRAING: talking for the sake of it
SEINE: a large fishing net
WASHICONGS: plimsoles, or sneakers
BELA: a type of dance like a quadrille
FLAMBEAUX: a petrol bomb used to provide light
CASA BALL: a sweet like a gobstopper or jawbreaker
BUISING: abusing
DISCOVERY DAY: a public holiday to celebrate
Columbus' landing (not observed since independence)
GALLERY WIT: showing off
COPRA: a fibrous matter that is a by-product of the
coconut

ACT TWO

JAB-JAB: a type of demon
TULUM: a sweet made with coconut and molasses
SAGA BOY: a flashy fellow
JUMBIE: a type of ghost

WAJANK: a hooligan
PLAY MAS: to go crazy
MAMA POOLS: a simpleton
MAMAGUYING/PAPAGUYING: to make fun of

ACT THREE

CRAPEAUX SMOKE HE PIPE: your fate is sealed
TOTIE: penis
BAZODEE: crazy
PUT GOAT MOUTH ON HIM: to wish someone bad luck
SOUKINGYA: a vampire-like demon
HEFFEA: a fellow to be respected by other men
BUSH BATH: a folk cure for bad luck
TOCO: a village and beach on the north coast
CHIP CHIP SOUP: a soup made of seashells
CARONI CANE: sugar cane grown in Caroni
SAN-E-MAN-E-TEH: without humanity
BRUSHING WOMAN: having sex with a woman
CARITE: a fish
PIROGUES: a open-topped boat
MY KNOCK'S IN: my luck's in (derived from the game of marbles)

ACT ONE

(A fishing village in Mayaro on the east coast of Trinidad— a rum shop. Evening. A counter. Tables. Chairs. Bags of rice stacked on one side. A door leading to room inside. Large, main, propped-up window. Shelves of bottles on wall behind counter.)

(PEGGY, of African origin, is writing on counter.)

PEGGY: And a pair a good sapats, wit strong rubber, no bicycle type ting, but motor car, a hear dem is de bess. A fine lice comb, six yards a cotton print either flowers or just print, yes, an a wide-brim straw hat for a wedding, all dis....

(STANLEY enters.)

STANLEY: He not here.

PEGGY: Yer see him. *(Addresses letter to)* Mister Shafieek Mohammed, Merchant. Marine Square, Port of Spain.

STANLEY: I en see him on de road, dats why.

PEGGY: How you go see him? *(Licks stamps, puts them on envelope)* You is a bat? De road dark like night, he coming doh.

STANLEY: Ah was outside yer no. Staning up dey. Ah didn't want ter come in, but a taught you would get vex if a didn't come in ter say howdy.

PEGGY: *(Putting letter in envelope)* Well, yer come in, sit down ner. He joining up with he pardners Phil and dem, a whole side a dem going ter de wake.

STANLEY: Yes, a hear bout it but dat too far ter go in de night.

PEGGY: Well, he an he pardners going an guess who have ter stay an keep it open, yer want anyting.

STANLEY: Just a sweet drink would do.

PEGGY: Yer fraid yer get drunk.

STANLEY: *(Pays)* No, a just. *(She gives him the bottle.)* Thanks.

PEGGY: We doh sell no bad rum here yer 'no.

STANLEY: A 'no, a 'no, is just not Saturday, da is all.

PEGGY: A see, is a good ting. Everybody not like you, we would only open Saturday.

STANLEY: I drink on Sunday too.

PEGGY: Oh yes a forget—we get a loada rice dis morning yer 'no, an he wasn't even here ter help unload. He say he went to buy a dog to keep me company.

STANLEY: Look, wen we get married, I go do most a de heavy lifting an glass cleaning.

PEGGY: How you so sure I go marry you?

STANLEY: But yer family agree is a good match, my bit a property an yours go make sense, a write de Registrar General, all we waiting for now, is de forms.

PEGGY: Yer 'no dey had a time in dis country wen black people wasn't allowed ter get married, now dey have ter write away an get forms ter write in, you feel some big-shot civil servant in Port of Spain go study we, an send back form, you tink dey even 'no whey dis place is? I do see why we can do like everybody an...

STANLEY: Peggy—a told yer it have ter be...

PEGGY: I 'no, church an ting—

STANLEY: Yes!

PEGGY: —me en 'no why. You want dis big church ting, none a we does go ter church only if somebody dead, or a christening or someting.

STANLEY: Dis village en big, but it growing, longtime it only had three fishing boat, now is a dozen, we didn't have no post office, now we have one.

PEGGY: You call dat 2-by-2 a post office? Yer have to hold an election, for the people to get out.

STANLEY: It does take letters.

PEGGY: So Mayaro is de Capital a de Western World.

STANLEY: Look, I own three a dem fishing boat an every week de catch growing. I 'no prosperity wen I see it, an wit prosperity comes respectability. We have ter set de example.

PEGGY: You telling me 'bout respectability, I can walk down de road wit out some saga boy whistling an calling out how big he yam is, wanting to 'no if I want ter come in he patch an see it, an dis is day time yer 'no, day time, I en go tell yer wat go happen at night.

STANLEY: Well ignore it an....

PEGGY: Of course a ignore it.

STANLEY: An next time it happen take he name an tell me I go fix him. If he fishing for me I go put a stop ter it.

PEGGY: Is all right fer you ter talk bout big talk, but is I have ter stay here lock up at night an have all kinda ting going on outside. Especially wen dem ole nigger get two rum in dem.

STANLEY: Well I woulda stay fer while wit yer, but yer 'no how people an dem does talk, a could ask Mama Benin ter look in.

PEGGY: Dat obeah woman, she go only frighten me more.

STANLEY: No, is just dat. When a walk past number 5 Coconut Tree dis evening, dey had dis feller lying down next ter it, drunk an cussing everybody who pass.

PEGGY: Wat he was saying?

STANLEY: I en go repeat de exact words, but take my word for it he was cussing, yer fadder dis, yer fadder dat, an de look in he eye it was fierce....

PEGGY: You sure is drunk? He drunk? Or some horse knock him down?

STANLEY: He sound drunk, an I wasn't going looking ter see for meself—suppose he jump up an lock my neck an tief my money. What woulda happen. I go tell you wha woulda happen, dey would be no wedding da is wat, cause I woulda spend six months in hospital an de doctor bill woulda cripple me.

PEGGY: You really have wedding on your mind eh, yer can't wait ter get in here an make yourself sweet an prosperous.

STANLEY: Peggy how you could say dat.

PEGGY: A could say it, it easy. I never meet a man like you, you so big an have all dese ambitious ideas under yer hat, an you hear a man lying down on de ground like he in a pain, an you walk off an left him dey. Night or no night at least yer coulda call out an see if he wanted assistance or someting.

STANLEY: It was evening.

PEGGY: Worse yet! An is you go' protect me? Well if dey fine him dead in de morning next ter number 5 Coconut Tree, a hope you go have a good story fer de magistrate, because he go want ter 'no how nobody ah see or hear notting, especially somebody who own number 5 Coconut Tree.

STANLEY: Oh, God, Peggy, a didn't tink a dat.

PEGGY: A 'no you didn't tink a dat, a 'no wat you tink a, a tell you already.

STANLEY: Oh, God, Peggy, yer hard, ya 'no? Do tell nobody I see him, or mention to anybody, he might sober heself up and go on he way, like nottin happen, a tink a hear him mumble someting bout Manzanilla, he probaly on he way dere already, so, no need ter mention anyting, not even ter yer fadder, because yer 'no he an de boys go give me a hard picong, a beg yer.

PEGGY: Doh beg. I en make up me mind yet.

STANLEY: A hear dem coming. Wat yer say?

PEGGY: I en say notting.

MEN: *(Off, singing)* Take me, take me
I am feeling lonely
Take me back to los Si Ros
But do le me madder 'no.

(MEN enter: PEGGY's father, PHIL, and JIM—they are poor fishermen.)

PHIL and JIM: Evening Miss Peggy.

PEGGY: Evening.

MIKEY: All yer sit down ner, an fire one. Peggy a bottle a White Label an.... Stanley, yer firing?

STANLEY: No tanks Mikey, Saturday fer me.

MIKEY: Tree glasses den.

(PEGGY brings bottle and glasses.)

PEGGY: Wha happen de wake en go have enough rum ter drink, all yer have ter tak precaution.

MIKEY: Dis daughter a mine have a mouth like a sting ray. Peggy yer 'no de boys an me have ter start off on de right foot. We car walk in de wake an everybody merry and we not, we go never catch up.

PEGGY: A see is catching up, yer catching up.

PHIL: *(Laughs)* So Mister Stanley wen is de wedding?

STANLEY: Ar, soon, soon. Dese tings doh happen out a de blue yer 'no.

JIM: *(Laughing)* No, yer have ter bait yer hook Mister Stanley.

STANLEY: Yes, yes. I doh 'no wat yer mean.

MIKEY: Wha is all dis Mister Stanley business? I taught we come here ter drink, not carry on parish council meeting.

PHIL: No, we only asking about bout de coming nuptuals.

PEGGY: Why you so interested in nuptuals? You live wit a woman fer ten years, you ever talk to she bout nuptuals?

JIM: Facts, facts.

PHIL: A was just tinking wat kinda present, a have ter get all yer.

JIM: Yes, yes, present or presence.

PHIL: Both, both.

PEGGY: You better make sure you have coconut, before you start make sugar cake.

PHIL: Good, good.

STANLEY: Is all right, Peggy I can take care a meself. Dis en go be o drunk an fall down wedding wit gallon a food an gallon a rum in ar yard. Yer go have plates ter eat outa. Yer hear dat.

MIKEY: De boy right, dats why a pick him!

PEGGY: I'd like ter see de tree, yer do dat from.

MIKEY: A bit force ripe, but da is all.

STANLEY: Better force ripe, dan rotten eh.

PHIL: A hear a joke! Jim, you hear a joke?

JIM: Yes, a tink so.

PHIL: Stanley.

STANLEY: Wat?

PHIL: You, you just tell a joke, Stanley.

STANLEY: Me?

PHIL: Yes. Jim, didn't you just hear Stanley tell a joke?

JIM: Yes. A did, a tink a did. Yes, a sure now a did, it was a joke. Yes, a real joke.

PHIL: We should carry him down de wake an cheer up everybody.

STANLEY: Ah no tanks, I....

JIM: Even poor Freddie might raise up from de dead an laugh too, wha yer say, Stanley?

STANLEY: No tanks. I going home an have a good night's sleep.

PEGGY: An all a all yer should do dat too, present company included, a could just see de tree a all yer, staggering down de dark road, bouncing into ditch after ditch, an staggering back doing de same ting.

PHIL: Is not de reaching is de joy, is de travelling.

JIM: Facts, facts.

PEGGY: Joy fer who, is I have ter lock up, an clean up, while you go off all night ter old talk an fill yer belly wit free rum.

MIKEY: Yer fadder have he reputation ter keep up girl, I car go down ter a wake an doh drink notting, apart from insulting Freddie newly arrived widow, tink a de wasted journey.

PEGGY: Explain dat one ter me.

JIM: Yea, me too, me too.

MIKEY: It simple.

PEGGY: If a was half way in de bottle like you a wouldn't ask.

JIM: But it only....

MIKEY: Jim, is like dis, if I go down dere or any body go down dere, an stay shorter dan it take dem ter go, dere, dey en really dere.

JIM: Yes.

PEGGY: Yes, a 'no some ting was simple, but it en me, you doh 'no de tings does go on out side dis shop at night cause yer never here, but is man jaming up woman an de house shaking, or man owe man money an en want te pay an is pulling cutlass an chopping an screaming an blood in de daybreak. No, you out simple.

MIKEY: But you is a big woman now.

JIM: Facts, facts.

MIKEY: Yer 'no how man is. A spend me whole life giving yer a example, yer have a man, if yer fraid, tell him, dat is why a pick him, is time he take over.

STANLEY: Me do wat, if I stay here late, it mean I have ter go home late, an dat—

PHIL: Go be late.

STANLEY: Yes.

JIM: How much late is dat.

PHIL: Two.

JIM: No three, two fer him, one fer you.

PHIL: Fact, fact.

MIKEY: Lord, wat kind man you is. I giving you a free hand wit me daughter, a clear road, no stop sign.

PEGGY: Go on, yer going good.

MIKEY: Is true, you 'no how much men would jump a de opportunity.

PEGGY: I 'no.

MIKEY: But he doh 'no. Yer is a man or a manhole? Wat in yer veins? Blood or bilgewater? All you tink bout is making money. If yer 'no de haggle paggle dis man have wit me before we agree to engagement. I bet he have Chinese blood in him.

MIKEY: Yer see, look at me, I have a business but I do let it rule my life.

PEGGY: A looking.

MIKEY: Stay out a dis Peggy, dis is man-ter-man talk.

PEGGY: Which is which?

MIKEY: I want gran children yer 'no.

PEGGY: Have dem ner.

STANLEY: A 'no wat yer mean mister Mikey.

MIKEY: No mister, I is Mikey.

STANLEY: But, an a will do me best not ter let yer down, after all yer go ter so much trouble ter pick me.

PEGGY: Why I doh go wit Phil and Jim an leave de both a all yer here, an all yer could have all de gran children all yer want.

STANLEY: A have ter go, a just have ter go, a shouldn't be here.

MIKEY: Who say dat, I say who should be here. I is still man in my own house, doh mind Peggy.

STANLEY: Look, a really doh want ter be rude ter yer hospitality but, wen a come up dis evening day had dis feller cussing an carrying on. An he might be still out dey an I en want ter get tie up in no court case, an all yer en going my way so.

MIKEY: Wat feller, me an see no feller.

STANLEY: Well I see him an if you had see him you woulda 'no wat a mean, ask Peggy, so I going. (Goes)

MIKEY: Wha he talking bout feller, child? Wat feller?

JIM: Yer 'no Stanley, he must be sell some shark an say is cavali.

PHIL: Or cavali, an say is kingfish. (Laughs)

MIKEY: Nar, he look serious.

PHIL: We too. (Laughs. STANLEY comes half in doorway.)

STANLEY: Mikey, Mikey de feller, de feller a was telling yer bout, he, he in de middle a de road, an a can't pass now.

MIKEY: So wat yer want me ter do, build a bridge over him?

STANLEY: He coming here, an he 'no I leave him lying down alone.

(Someone coughs outside. KEN enters—African origin—20s, tired and dirty.)

KEN: Evening.

MEN: Evening.

(KEN goes to counter.)

KEN: I'll have a eights please Miss. (Pays)

PEGGY: *(Serving, pours rum into small glass)* You one a de fellers building de new road, de one from Rio Claro.

KEN: No. I en build no road, a walk it, a was walking all day, if a had fine a road a woulda walk on it but a come trough de coconut.

MIKEY: Da is a long way, like de sun beat yer, take a seat ner.

KEN: Tanks. *(Goes to sit)* Yer does get plenty police an ting coming here.

MIKEY: Dey 'no better dan dat. Dis place is behind God's back. We does settle we our business here. Dis place is fer drinking. Outside is fer fishing an fighting, we doh need dem.

KEN: Da is alright den.

MIKEY: Yer want ter drink, fish, or fight?

KEN: Drink, Sir.

MIKEY: Yer see Stanley.

STANLEY: Leave me outa dis.

MIKEY: But doh get us wrong yer 'no, dis en no packoti house.

PEGGY: A glad ter hear yer say dat, you'd make a funny-looking madame.

MIKEY: So why you ask bout police an ting, dey want yer for something?

KEN: Day want a lot a people.

MIKEY: Yes. I hear dey en have no work in town.

KEN: I en from town.

MIKEY: No I en tink so, you is a land man.

KEN: Yes, so?

MIKEY: Rice or cane, someting tell me cane, but a tink is rice.

KEN: Tink again.

MIKEY: Cane, a 'no it was cane. Yer tief cane an sell it.

KEN: I was tinking bout someting different an more serious.

PEGGY: Dey never pull down yer pants and beat yer in school? How come yer en 'no wat you do?

MIKEY: Even Basil de Boobalee 'no de difference between tiefing an....

KEN: I look like a tief ter you? If my fadder could her you now he'd turn in his grave, he coulda buy up dis whole place from de top of he pocket, an still have change.

PEGGY: So is aristocracy we have, excuse de table cloth, it en linen.

MIKEY: Let de man talk, ner, give him another eight, dis one on me. So if it en tief yer tief, is bigger dan dat den.

KEN: Deres big an big.

JIM: He look like de kinda feller who would grab a girl in de dark an....

KEN: Me, not me. Da is one ting I would never do. Not even if it was Hedy Lammar.

PHIL: Yer let me down Jim, yer en hear de man say he fadder was a money man, an now he on hard times. He family rob him a he rightful inheritance, I see a picture once where....

MIKEY: Yer wicked uncle.

KEN: Nar man.

PHIL: Yer stepfather.

KEN: Never had one.

JIM: Yer elder half brodder.

KEN: Neither.

MIKEY: Well who den, yer drink it an spen it on one a dem girl on Green Corner.

PEGGY: Who story it is we trying ter fine out here?

KEN: None a dem tings, man, all yer does watch too much pictures yer 'no. I en tinking bout none a dem tings.

PHIL: Well you is a real fathom, boy. I no, yer grab one a dem English sailor an take he shillings.

KEN: I wouldn't grab one a dem for a dollar much less a shilling.

JIM: He's a good-looking feller, three women wanted ter marry him an he couldn't say no. I hear a lot a feller in town does do dat, an wen it get out dey have ter run.

KEN: Nar I en married, not even one, much less.

PEGGY: All yer en see he en do nottin, he just garraying with he drink.

MIKEY: But he must be do someting, no man en go run from he home so. I can't go to de wake an en 'no de story. It must have a ending.

PEGGY: Look, if yer en rob, or tief or kill or do notting bad, wat yer run for. Yer feel like running, tell dem, yer en do notting.

KEN: Notting you call it? Notting? You 'no how much jail waiting on me. De hangman tying de rope now for me dis minute.

PEGGY: You only say dat ter get attention, you en do notting. A nice-looking boy like you, you wouldn't harm a fly would you?

KEN: He wasn't a fly and how you 'no? How you 'no wat a nice-looking feller like me would do?

PEGGY: How I 'no, a go tell yer how I 'no, I spen my whole life listening ter fellers like you come in here an old talk all night, so if yer doh want me ter do *(Picking up broom)* wat I do ter dem yer better....

KEN: *(Turning around and putting up his hands)* I kill me ole man. Me ole man, a kill him, last Saturday a do it.

PEGGY: You kill yer fadder?

KEN: Yes.

PHIL: *(Drawing back)* But you is a hell of a feller.

JIM: *(Also drawing back)* I second dat.

MIKEY: But da is a hell of a ting ter do, man. Dat is a straight rope and trap door job fer you. You musta have plenty reason ter do dat, but even so....

KEN: He was a wicked man, an de older he get de more wickeder he get. A reach me limit.

PEGGY: Yer shoot him, or poison him wit ground-up glass in a cow's milk?

KEN: Poison is too sneaking fer me an I en have no license for no gun, an if yer get catch wit one an no license is jail.

MIKEY: A switch blade, a hear dem tings does just fly out an into de body.

KEN: Dat is fer dem pimp an pickpocket in town.

PEGGY: You didn't hang im, like wen he was drunk, yer get he belt buckle an hook it trough a beam?

KEN: Nar. A had a cutlass. A just raise it up an drop de blade on de edge a he skull, here *(Shows)* an he dead like a ripe mango, squash like one too, blood all over de place, an not a sound come outa him.

MIKEY: *(Pours drink for Ken)* An how come you en get catch feller, yer bury too.

KEN: Yes, right dey an den a bury him, in de cane field.

MIKEY: A 'new you was a cane man.

PHIL: Fact, fact.

KEN: We was right dey, cutting cane, an...

MIKEY: An de police or overseers never came after you, a whole week dey must....

KEN: Not a sign a dem, an is de road I walk on, a only come trough de coconuts because de road run out.

PHIL: Facts, facts. Wat a feller you is. Dey en go come after a feller like you, dey no better! Because if you turn, dey getting it too.

MIKEY: Why not? An which part yer bury him?

KEN: *(Suspicious)* Oh, some part a de country Mister Rum Shop Owner, some part.

JIM: He en giving notting away, sly mongoose.

PHIL: He right too.

PEGGY: We could do wit somebody wit dat kinda brains round here, at least wen a say put de white dey an put de red rum dey a go fine dem....

MIKEY: Wat?

PEGGY: An yer en go even have ter pay a dollar, fifty cents go do.

MIKEY: Girl, wat you saying?

PEGGY: A saying he here is we new bottle boy.

PHIL: Dat right, de police fraid im, an dey en go come round here ter see wat hours yer stay open, or even if yer license up ter date! In fact, yer en go even need license now! He go just raise he hand an run dem.

JIM: An all yer money an ting.

MIKEY: Wat money?

JIM: Mikey, we 'no yer have some change put away, it go be safe now—wen de word get round people go wipe de foot before dey come in here—any man who would kill he fadder is a man ter respect.

MIKEY: Yer sure?

JIM: Fact man, facts.

PEGGY: Is true! An if he was under dis roof, dem could kill one another outside dey. I go sleep like a top, an you could go out an galavant wen yer like.

MIKEY: But I does do dat.

PHIL: But not wit a clean conscience.

MIKEY: True, true.

JIM: He does worry about yer, yer 'no.

PEGGY: A 'no.

MIKEY: An you en going to say if you madder was alive she would die of a heart attack.

PEGGY: No. A wouldn't have de cause to.

MIKEY: Fifty cents yer say?

PEGGY: Even de Lord en go give yer a cheaper forgiveness.

MIKEY: How all dat sound to you, young feller?

KEN: It sound good. Just de kinda ting I was tinking of.

MIKEY: An yer could work hard?

KEN: Yes.

PHIL: After de cane fields dis go be like a stroll round de Memorial Park.

MIKEY: Hold yer horses an you go do wat de girl tell yer an no sly drinking.

KEN: Not a drop witout permission.

STANLEY: After wat he do, yer en tink it kinda dangerous ter have him here?

PEGGY: Nobody en ask you your opinion yer 'no.

STANLEY: But he chop he fadder....

PEGGY: Yer better watch out or your tongue might get it too! An you, young feller, as yer see, it en go be back-breaking work like pulling seine, an I en a bad cook, so....

KEN: An yer say de police doh come here.

MIKEY: De only one is on horseback, an de horse does ride he home. He sleeping all de time, an wen he hear how bad you is he go pass here like a full tram car.

JIM: *(Gets up)* Matter fix, yer daughter go get she nights sleep, wit a man who kill he old man guarding she an yer property, Mikey, so le we go down de road before dey drink up all de rum an is only burn rice an peas left.

MIKEY: *(Up at door)* An you, young feller, wat yer want us ter call yer?

KEN: Ken, short for Kenneth.

MIKEY: Alright, Ken short for Kenneth, a leave me prosperity an daughter in yer safe hands, an a go see all yer in de morning.

PEGGY: Go ner.

KEN: All yer have a good time man.

(Song. Calypso.)

STANLEY: *(Lingering at the door)* Am, Peggy, yer want me ter keep company a bit longer, a could yer 'no.

PEGGY: An yer say yer was in a hurry ter go.

STANLEY: Well tings change now, a was fraid for me, but now is you.

PEGGY: Doh worry bout me, I go be alright. Yer didn't want ter stay wen a wanted yer, now a doh want yer, yer want ter.

STANLEY: If a bounce into Mama Benin a go send....

PEGGY: Go ner, man. Yer en see I have ter close up. *(Pushes him out, closes door)* Boy, dat man is a cross. Why yer do lie down on de rice bags an take it there? You must be dead.

KEN: *(Goes over, taking off plimsoles)* Yes. Tanks. Dese washicongs stick on ter me foot, is de sweat yer no.

PEGGY: Yes, yer family an dem must a have plenty land an ting ter give you a name like Kenneth. Is de first time I hear a name like dat. A hope de bags en too hard on yer back.

KEN: No, dey fine, fine. *(Patting them)* Yes, cane fields far as yer eye could see, en even farder.

PEGGY: A taught so, yer family musta be pleased ter have a good-looking son like you, ter have ter give up all dat.

KEN: Me?

PEGGY: Yes!

KEN: Yes, yes, a see. Yes, yes.

PEGGY: Wha happen? De girls an dem blind, whey yer come from?

KEN: Dey not blind, no, not blind, smart. Deceitful an untrustworthy, but not blind, no.

PEGGY: Dey must be, but somebody musta tell yer, yer musta been giving yer story ter de young ones an even de old ones too.

KEN: I en tell a soul wat go on, until ternight, yer hear Peggy, an is tiredness an de rum make me do dat, a tink if you an yer fadder wasn't such nice people a woulda start regretting it now, but especially you.

PEGGY: Me?

KEN: Yes.

PEGGY: I make yer do wat?

KEN: You make me feel safe. An a fella could let down he guard an it go be alright if a do it, an you put in all dem good words fer me.

PEGGY: I do all dat?

KEN: You doh 'no, because you was doing it, but I notice.

PEGGY: I bet you say dat ter every petticoat you come across, on de line or on de body.

KEN: A tell yer, no one till ternight, get ter hear my secret. I en see no one in days especially no one like you. It was only swamp, dirt track, corbeaux, an stray dogs, much less nice-looking girls like you, sea bathing—

PEGGY: Well boy, is a good ting you tired yer hear or else you would never run out a sweet talk ternight.

KEN: *(Gets off bags, goes close to hear)* A hope yer doh take offense, but....

PEGGY: No. Why?

KEN: I'd like ter ask you a personal question. Tell me if a too fast or box me face.

PEGGY: Ask me ner. I look like some Sunday-school teacher ter you?

KEN: Yer married ter anybody?

PEGGY: Me. I look like I married? I like my freedom too much. Dat Stanley have it on he brain but le him keep it dey. A was never good at darning socks, or turning shirt collars.

KEN: Me neither. I just like you!

PEGGY: Look, I never killed my fadder. I would be too fraid ter do dat, but boy, sometimes he does get me so vex, a could. It must a been de same wit you.

KEN: Ahm.

PEGGY: I en say it was easy, but yer do it.

KEN: It wasn't easy! We used ter get on like house on fire, but he meet dis woman.

PEGGY: Ah.

KEN: Soon as a see im put on a suit, a 'new someting was up an den a see him bathe by de stand pipe, with soap!

PEGGY: Yes.

KEN: An he bring she home, an from after dat, he wouldn't let me rest in peace. How I taking up too much room an a eating more dan a planting an on an on he went every time he come back from seeing she.

PEGGY: Yes. He didn't 'no wat was in store fer him.

KEN: No. Nobody 'no, up to dis day a kill im. Nobody 'no. I was de nicest feller in de whole a Trinidad. A would drink wit de boys. I never used ter give nobody no trouble.

PEGGY: *(Getting out bedspread)* Maybe is de women an dem who start yer off, wen dey notice yer is a man, yer start waiting ter act like one.

KEN: No a tell yer. Nobody was noticing me in de fields, woman, girls, cow or goat.

PEGGY: An I taught you was dis big hot boy, just snapping he fingers an have de world at he feet. Here.

(PEGGY brings enamel cup of tea and bread and cheese.)

PEGGY: Get dis down yer.

KEN: De world at me feet? A wish so! It was rock, or big snake after I done clear canal, an dig trench from morning till sunset. It was just me, an de cane, yer ever look down a cane field an all yer could see is rows an rows a cane?

PEGGY: Yes, like de coconut.

KEN: Worse! Noting ter give yer a joke or make yer laugh. De only joy I had was listening ter de birds, an catching dem, an at night a used ter go down by de lagoon an catch crab. Dat was nice.

PEGGY: Nice you call dat, a big man like you, going by yerself ter catch crab?

KEN: Yes. Dat was happiness for me, real happiness. You doh 'no wat its like ter see de full moon come up an de crabs come out to belá, is like a fete fer dem, dey meet, exchange greetings, chat, dance wit one another an have a meal too. All wit de moonlight shining on dey backs, making dem change color, is a sin ter put flambeaux in de face an grab dem for de pot. An after a fill a crocus bag, I'd take off me short pants an swim in de lagoon, an as a dive in, de million an one lights in de water would just burst an be two million an one.

PEGGY: Why yer fadder didn't go wit yer?

KEN: He? Dat ole scamp? He say only madman go out in de full moon an if a doh watch out de moon go take wat brains he give me. No, he'd be sleeping off a drink, snoring like a bad fiddler an cussing an buising in he sleep.

PEGGY: Lord.

KEN: Even you woulda fraid him wen he wake up, a doh 'no wen he was worse sleeping or waking. I see dat man kick a dog til it just lie down.

PEGGY: He musta been a true, true devil. I on dis earth twenty an someting years now an notting would ever bring me ter treat my fadder so.

KEN: If yer had mine it would, a tell yer, it was me working de cane while he sit back on a tree stump an complaining, saying a cut de ditch crooked an a plant de root too shallow, an is my fault it en rain ter day, and dat was my cross till a couldn't take no more last Saturday an drop de cutlass on im.

PEGGY: (Putting hand on his shoulder) Well, he resting in peace now an your cross get put down. Yer en go carry none here, is time a nice feller like you get he reward an grace on dis earth.

KEN: Is more dan time, a man like me who en do nobody no harm, but who en fraid nobody, my back broad yer....

(There is a knock.)

KEN: Oh Lord, a sure is de police, a taught yer tell me....

PEGGY: (Motions him shush) Who's dat? All yer doh 'no people does sleep, it late.

VOICE: It's me, Peggy.

PEGGY: Me who?

VOICE: Mama Benin.

PEGGY: *(Getting up)* You sit down dey an cut yer bread an cheese, an play sleepy because all she want is one sign you want ter garray an she go set up all night.

(KEN sits up eating, back to door. PEGGY opens door.)

PEGGY: Wat yer want Mama Bénin, yer run outa candles, it late yer no, if yer fall asleep yer could come and get dem in de morning.

MAMA BENIN: *(Entering, 40's)* No chile. I have enough candle ter read forty book and forty psalms with, an de sleep en hit me yet. No, a pass into yer young feller Stanley, an he tell me yer have dis outsider feller who was moaning and wailing, an funny sound was coming out he mouth, so a say a better come and make sure yer had me protection.

PEGGY: Protection from wat? Yer see me half naked an he pouring white rum down my troat, yer en see a natural man, sit down an eat natural bread an drink natural milk in a mug.

MAMA BENIN: Yes, a see, but how natural is natural?

PEGGY: Well yer take my word fer it, an yer could tell dat ter Mister Stanley.

MAMA BENIN: I en passing him again ter night.

PEGGY: Yer en see he half-dead wit sleep, he couldn't even fine de button much less undo a blouse.

MAMA BENIN: A see wat yer say but, Mister Stanley say he doh charge me rent for two-room house as is only me, and dis feller here could take de edder room an de rent go stay de same.

PEGGY: Wen? Ternight?

MAMA BENIN: Yes, he say too, an I agree with im, dat a pure girl like you, can share de same roof wit a outsider feller! Doh take notting, Mister.

KEN: Notting taken.

MAMA BENIN: *(Smiles)* Well you look like a nice-looking feller, how come I hear all dose stories bout you? It musta been a really strong spirit dat make you shed blood, or yer didn't walk backward at de bridge.

KEN: I doh 'no.

MAMA BENIN: He so modest too, who would tink he had de pluck ter kill he ole man, eh.

PEGGY: *(At center, washing glasses)* Doh worry bout him, wen he ready he could hole he own wit any man in dis world, but yer en see he tired a travelling, is a week he walking, yer no, a hole week, so give him a fat chance ner.

MAMA BENIN: I go give him a chance till he finish eating. He could even belch, den we'll go over ter my place, yer go fine I easy ter get along wit, and if me cooking taste a bit different is fer yer own good, we have a lot in common.

KEN: You kill yer ole man?

PEGGY: Kill wat, he get a sore an she put a copper cent on it an de blood get poison, da is de kinda kill she kill an get fame and respect fer it, if yer wasn't so mean an put a whole penny he woulda dead sooner.

MAMA BENIN: He dead doh. Dats wat matters, not how! Anyway everybody no a woman who bury her children, get rid a she man, an knows de ways a de world, is better suited ter look after a man like you, dan a young girl who head go turn like a windmill every time a man give you a sweet eye.

PEGGY: You have de fastness ter say dat Mama Benin, wen yer almost lose yer breath running down de road ter see wat he look like.

MAMA BENIN: Who me? I just stroll pass like a lady on she Sunday afternoon jaunt, but is a good ting a happen by. Stanley was right. He musta hear de same ting in yer voice I hear. I is a woman too yer 'no, an I 'no dat look in yer eye, a man wit de fiercemess in him ter kill he ole man, doh need much hinting. *(Holding* KEN*)* So le we go young feller, yer must be had yer feast by now.

PEGGY: *(Grabs him)* He en going no where, hell or heaven or wat ever yer call yer spare room, he working here now. Bottle boy! Da is his work, I say so an me fadder say so, an nobody en tiefing him.

MAMA BENIN: Nobody en tiefing him, I make him free ter walk whey he want, no bottle boy in he right mind go sleep in a rum shop. Yer ever see a preacher sleep in he church? No. He have a right ter see my house, it right on de hill overlooking de bay an wen yer wake up in de morning....

PEGGY: Yes, see it in de morning Ken but pray it do rain because she roof have more holes dan a wire netting, an wen yer step over de dead dog an dead cat on she front step, look on she walls, an try wiping de dust off, is like it tatoo on wit age. An talking a age....

MAMA BENIN: Doh mine she, Ken. She trying ter make a good job a putting yer off an failing. No wat yer go see is a lonely woman tending ter she provision garden.

PEGGY: Tending is de right word, asks she wat herbs an spice she tend in dat garden, de whole village 'no, wen de bishop came here ter drive you out, you give him a soup ter eat and he walk out yer house saying he see he son who volunteer to go to France lying shot in de muddy trench wit rats having im fer souse. Ask anybody an wha bout dem fishermen who does line up outside she door like some ticket office.

MAMA BENIN: Lord, woman, yer mout bad. If slander was a sin yer'd be in hell dis minute. Yer hear how she

go on an yer only 'no she fer hours? Wha yer tink a
week go be like? A hope de Lord grow plenty wax in
yer ears.

PEGGY: Wha you listening ter her fer? Tell her ter go an
make a rounds.

MAMA BENIN: A going, but he coming too.

PEGGY: *(Shaking* KEN*)* Wha happen ter you? Yer sucking
casa ball? Talk ner.

KEN: *(To* MAMA BENIN*)* A sure yer have a nice
comfortable house, but a get bottle boy here an is here a
go stay.

PEGGY: Yer hear dat? Well we go see yer later den.

MAMA BENIN: Yer go send a ole lady like me out in de
dark by she self, knowing wat kinda demons out dere?
A could lie down on de odder rice bags Peggy an he
could take dose.

PEGGY: Wat yer mad or wat? Or yer tink I is? Is going
yer going an da is it. Alé, Alé.

MAMA BENIN: *(Wrapping shawl around shoulders)* Alright
a going. But you Peggy, a hope you don't get ole like
me an have people trow you out in de dark night.

PEGGY: I go manage.

MAMA BENIN: An you young fella, a wish yer all de
good tings yer deserve, but drunk or sober mind yer
business. If you tink is romance yer go get here doh
ferget, she only waiting. As he himself would tell yer,
ter marry up wit Stanley, she only want a man round
her fer de Discovery Day regatta, an ter gallery wit at
de fete. So if yer have cocoa in de sun yer look for rain.

*(*MAMA BENIN *exits.* PEGGY *locks door.)*

KEN: Wha was dat she say.

PEGGY: She say a lota ting. I doh pay no attention, gibberish an robber talk, da is all. Yer 'no dem bush people.

KEN: So all yer en getting married den.

PEGGY: Married wat? I wouldn't marry he if had twenty fishing boat an a school a kingfish swim into he net.

KEN: Well a glad ter hear dat. All yer celebrating discovery here.

PEGGY: Of course, you think we backward. We hold it every year. It go be good dis year, de fisherman does race, an pull, an have all kinda competition. We does sell more rum dat day den de whole year put together.

KEN: Yes.

PEGGY: See look, a put a cover on de bags fer yer. I hem it meself last week. I turning in now, a go see yer in de morning. Get yerself a good night's sleep. (PEGGY *goes in.*)

KEN: (*Calling out*) An tanks fer ternight.

(KEN *picks up bed cover and examines it. He talks to himself.*)

KEN: Even de rice bags go feel like a copra mattress tonight. (*He lies down and wriggles.*)

KEN: Once a get de bag moulded ter me body a go be out like a light. Well terday was a day an a half. A end up wit two women fighting over me for me company an a bottle boy work ter boot. You 'no a can help tinking a was a real slow coach not ter kill the fadder ages ago. (KEN *snores. Lights.*)

CURTAIN

ACT TWO

(The rum shop. Morning. Bright. KEN *is getting dressed: Shirt, khaki trousers, and white plimsoles.)*

KEN: *(To himself)* Boy, I never see so much rum in my whole life, and so much glasses. Ah 'no a go have ter wash dem but is still a lot. *(*KEN *goes behind the counter, stands and smiles as if serving customers.)* Well dis is de place ter be serving eights. Yes man, one eights coming up! A bottle a ginger ale ter chase? Somebody coming! Lord. *(*KEN *runs into back room.)*

(There is a knock at the door. A young girl enters, ALICE, *18ish.)*

ALICE: Nobody en here.

*(*IVY, *the same age as* ALICE, *enters. They both look around, wide-eyed.)*

IVY: Yer tink dey still in bed, wrap up.

ALICE: It too late fer dat now.

IVY: An it too early fer dem strolling.

ALICE: I feel dat Stanley was only papyshowing we. Dey en have no young feller here, nice or ugly.

IVY: *(Pointing to bed cover)* So who was sleeping dey? A jab-jab? Look, you could see de outline a he body. He look tall. Yer 'no wat dey say bout tall men, dey have...

ALICE: Ivy, yer mother go wash out yer mout with blue soap yer 'no.

IVY: Is true.

ALICE: Who tell you dat? A tall man?

IVY: No, I hear it. Wilma say, a tall feller show she...

ALICE: True, an wha she do? A bet she laugh an run off.

IVY: It shoulda run behind she. *(They laugh.)*

ALICE: One day dat Wilma go get wats coming ter she.

IVY: Me too!

ALICE: An me! *(They laugh.)* But dis is a real waste a time. We miss breakfast run down de road ter catch a glimpse of dis feller who kill he fadder, and he gone.

IVY: Yes girl, but at least we see where he lie down.

ALICE: Yes, dat is someting.

IVY: An de cover dat cover him.

ALICE: Le me smell it. De say yer could tell wat a man like by he smell yer 'no.

IVY: Who tell yer dat?

ALICE: Wilma, she say.

IVY: Le me have a smell. Hmm. It strong! Wat Wilma say if it strong?

ALICE: Dat he strong too.

IVY: *(Goes to door of back room and listens)* She was right, an he kill he fadder!

ALICE: Dis is de last time I get papy show yer hear, de last time! Last week dey tell we a Indian feller was charming snakes an eating fire, an wha happen wen we run up by de junction?

IVY: We see de ashes.

ALICE: But we en see no trills. Dat Peggy must be have she rudeness wit him, an send him.

IVY: *(Whispers)* Alice, shush!

ALICE: Shush yerself, I en no foul.

IVY: Somebody here, inside. *(Pushing door)* Excuse me. Morning, Mr. Mikey, Miss Peggy—is a feller!

ALICE: Wat!

(KEN comes out as the girls back off.)

KEN: All yer looking fer Peggy?

IVY: No.

ALICE: Yes.

KEN: Wat? Make up yer mind.

ALICE: Mister Mikey. We wanted ter 'no if he was still selling de bike.

IVY: Yes.

(KEN goes, picks up cover, folds, presses rice bag to remove shape.)

IVY: *(To ALICE)* Girl, you could lie.

KEN: Wat?

IVY: Notting. A have a sore troat.

KEN: Oh, I en 'no notting bout no bike.

ALICE: Is alright. We go wait till he come.

KEN: Peggy might 'no, but she gone ter get some eggs ter scramble.

IVY: Wilma say scrambled eggs good fer....

ALICE: Ivy, shush. Dis feller doh want ter 'no wat Wilma say. You 'no Wilma, Mister?

KEN: No.

ALICE: *(To IVY)* Yer see. Yer living here long?

KEN: No.

ALICE: Ah see.

IVY: Yer is a stranger den.

KEN: Yes.

IVY: Ah see.

ALICE: Yer like it here?

KEN: It en bad.

IVY: De people kinda ole fashion, but we going into ter Port of Spain one day.

KEN: Yes.

ALICE: You 'no Port of Spain, Mister?

KEN: No.

IVY: Ah see.

ALICE: Mister, yer doh mind if a ask yer a personal?

IVY: Alice, shush.

ALICE: Shush yerself!

IVY: How come you could ask but I can't?

ALICE: I older.

IVY: Only by a month.

ALICE: Dat is enough. Dis is de last time a bring yer wit me.

IVY: You didn't bring me, I bring you.

KEN: Wat it is yer wanted ter ask?

ALICE: See. *(To* IVY*)* Yes. You is de feller who kill he fadder?

KEN: Yes. Rest he soul.

(ALICE *takes bundle out of basket, thrusts it to* KEN.)

ALICE: Den dis is fer you. Take dem. Is two dozen a de best fresh-water oysters, Wilma say.

IVY: I didn't 'no you had dem.

ALICE: You doh 'no every ting bout me, yer 'no. Open de cloth yer go see dey big like a house an fulla juice an meat.

KEN: *(Opens cloth)* Yes, dey big.

(IVY takes cloth out of basket, thrusts it to KEN.)

IVY: An dis is fer you Mister. Fresh tulum, a make it dis morning wit new molasses. Wilma say molasses....

ALICE: I didn't 'no you make dem! Wen...?

IVY: You doh 'no everyting bout me, Miss Alice. De molasses go give yer back yer strength after last night.

ALICE: Ivy.

IVY: Ivy wat. De feller do a lot last night.

ALICE:. Ivy.

IVY: A lot of travelling an walking.

ALICE: Or.

KEN: Yes. A could still feel de aches.

IVY: Yer see.

ALICE: Yes, so how long yer here for.

KEN: I....

(MAMA BENIN enters.)

MAMA BENIN: Alice Henry an Ivy Hunt. Wat in de Lord's name all yer doing here dis hour a de morning?

(Girls giggle.)

MAMA BENIN: Eh.

IVY: But he's de feller who kill he fadder.

MAMA BENIN: I 'no he's de feller who kill he fadder. Why yer tink I come here? I come ter take him ter de regatta, an all yer all dress up ter go an tantalize de boys, wha all yer doing here?

ALICE: Mama Benin, if you enter him a bet he go beat everybody. I go bet on him.

IVY: Me too.

MAMA BENIN: All yer could bet yer bet, but he en go beat nobody if he waste strength talking ter all yer. *(Taking presents from* KEN*)* Yer eat yet?

KEN: Not yet.

MAMA BENIN: *(To girls)* Yer see wha a tell all yer. Now go an look in de back an see wat dey have fer breakfast. *(Girls exit.* MAMA BENIN *turns to* KEN*.)* An you. Come an sit down here instead a grinning like a Cheshire Cat. An tell me someting.

KEN: Peggy might come back.

MAMA BENIN: Doh worry about Miss High-an-mighty Peggy. She have more fish dan she can fry. I want ter 'no wha happen wen yer chop de ole man, lighten flash?

KEN: No.

MAMA BENIN: A hen dat never lay drop half a dozen eggs?

KEN: No.

MAMA BENIN: Wha happen ter yer man, something musta happen, tink, tink. I 'no! Yer see bat fly past.

KEN: It was day time.

MAMA BENIN: Well tell me den.

KEN: We was in de cane, clearing, an....

MAMA BENIN: An a two-head snake crawl out an tip he hat. Wha kinda hat he was wearing.

KEN: My ole man never wear hat.

MAMA BENIN: Not yer old man, de snake.

KEN: Dere wasn't no snake.

MAMA BENIN: Yer not telling de story right yer 'no.

KEN: A trying, Mama Benin.

MAMA BENIN: Call me Mama.

KEN: Alright, Mama.

MAMA BENIN: Dats better.

KEN: Tanks. Yes, a was clearing cane an he was just giving me a hard time an telling me wen a go get married an move out.

(Girls enter, carrying food for KEN.)

MAMA BENIN: Ah, a woman.

KEN: Yes, dis Indian girl.

(Girls listen.)

KEN: She fadder had dead an leave she a piece a land.

MAMA BENIN: Is dat where yer get de idea from.

KEN: Nar, he dead natural.

MAMA BENIN: De best way.

KEN: He wanted me ter court she fer she piece a land.

MAMA BENIN: An why yer didn't. Dem Indian girl like Creole man.

KEN: I didn't want ter.

ALICE: Dey could cook good roti and look after a man.

KEN: Dat's wat he say.

MAMA BENIN: Alice Henry dis is my story.

ALICE: Sorry Mama Benin.

MAMA BENIN: Go on.

KEN: She would end up looking after he, not me.

IVY: Is dat why yer didn't court her.

KEN: No.

MAMA BENIN: Ivy Hunt, a tell yer friend an I'll tell yer, dis is my story.

IVY: But we cook de breakfast.

MAMA BENIN: Ivy, yer want ter get married an have a lot a healthy children?

IVY: Sorry Mama.

MAMA BENIN: Go on now.

KEN: Wat.

MAMA BENIN: Yer was saying yer didn't want ter marry she.

KEN: Oh yes. She would come an bring me tings she cook ter taste. Yer right, de rotis was sweet.

MAMA BENIN: But wha I can understand is why yer never....

ALICE: Me neither.

IVY: Me too.

MAMA BENIN: She was ugly.

KEN: No, she had de biggest eyes like midnight, de smoothest skin like water, an long black shining hair down ter she waist.

ALICE: Yer hear dat.

IVY: I hear.

MAMA BENIN: An why, tell me ner man, before me brain bust out me head.

IVY: It like a Saturday serial, eh.

(MAMA BENIN *looks at* IVY.)

IVY: Sorry Mama.

KEN: Mama, ladies, girls, I en 'no if all yer go believe dis but....

MAMA BENIN: Yes, yes.

(The girls stretch over.)

KEN: A didn't love her.

(The girls scream and then sit.)

ALICE: Jeezam ages.

IVY: Dat is man, oh yes.

ALICE: Man fer so.

MAMA BENIN: Yes, yes, ah see.

ALICE: Even you have ter praise dat, Mama.

MAMA BENIN: You watch yer steps Alice. I might look like a castle ter you, but I 'no wat love is.

KEN: No matter how sweet she was, she used ter wear a sari and she had de sweetest-looking navel peeping out, an a gold earring through she nose an a red spot on she forid.

MAMA BENIN: Yer still couldn't do it, eh.

(KEN shakes his head.)

ALICE: Doh tell we no more. Doh tell we no more. We see it, we see it.

KEN: A glad all yer see it, but yer see he didn't see it. He couldn't. De more a tell him is de more he call me names like Nancy Boy and Sailor Barrel.

IVY: Yer should a give 'im it dey.

KEN: A did.

IVY: Good.

KEN: A was bending down brushing an a say, look at dis, and he bend down, an I rise up an drop de cutlass on him an wen de blade hit de bone it ring like a church bell.

MAMA BENIN: Ah, a bell ring.

KEN: An a say rest in peace before I go, an he twitch ter de right an a turn ter face de sun—

MAMA BENIN: Ah de sun, de moon woulda been better but go on.

KEN: An a hit 'im another one fer luck, dis time de bell en ring it just went through flesh.

MAMA BENIN: One ring is enough.

KEN: An he drop, an a 'no he was gone forever.

MAMA BENIN: No turning back. Gone is gone.

KEN: Right.

ALICE: Well, wat a story. It better dan anyting I ever hear. All fer love.

IVY: Love is strong yer 'no.

ALICE: I 'no, I 'no.

IVY: It does move mountains.

ALICE: Yes. Faith too.

IVY: Is dat same fate dat send you here ter tell us dat story. Is a sign dat you have ter be here, wat yer say Alice.

ALICE: Yes fate. Fate bring you here ter meet Mama Benin fer a reason.

IVY: Ter marry wid she. Why yer doh give she a hug?

(IVY *puts* KEN's *arm around* MAMA BENIN.)

MAMA BENIN: Doh tease de boy, er.

(ALICE *gets a bottle and two glasses. She gives them to*
MAMA BENIN *and* KEN.)

ALICE: Any woman who bring out a great story in a
man is ter keep she forever. (*Pours from the bottle*) Drink
a toast to two a de best-matched people in de West
Indies. De heart and de souls, in one harmony. Drink,
drink ter slaves dat run off with cattle dey work for. Ter
de slaves who poisoned dey selves wen dey couldn't
take bondage no more, and ter de slaves a Hispañola
who rise up on de French an win de freedom, ter
Toussaint Louverture.

MAMA BENIN: Dat is a great toast, wat yer say Ken.

(MAMA BENIN *and* KEN *link arms and drink.* PEGGY *enters
with eggs. The girls jump back.* MAMA BENIN *stays.*)

PEGGY: (*To* ALICE *and* IVY) All yer, yer want someting.

ALICE: Yes.

IVY: No.

PEGGY: Make up yer mind.

ALICE: A came ter fine out if yer fadder was still selling
de bike.

PEGGY: Is bike yer want ter ride den.

ALICE: Yes.

PEGGY: I taught it was only donkey yer ride.

ALICE: A could pay fer it.

PEGGY: A sure yer could, see me fadder bout it. Next.

IVY: Daddy send me fer some tobacco.

PEGGY: Yer remember!

IVY: Yes.

PEGGY: (*Getting tobacco from shelf*) Six cents.

IVY: (*Looking in basket*) A ferget me purse.

PEGGY: Yer ferget a lot a tings. De first is, dis is not a Chinese shop. Six cents or no tobacco.

IVY: Oh God, Peggy. Doh make me have ter run home ter get it. Daddy go cut me tail.

PEGGY: Yer wasn't so worried bout yer tail a minute ago. (*To* MAMA BENIN) An you Mama Benin, what a could do fer you.

MAMA BENIN: A can tink a notten right now, but yer could send me over a quarter cake a blue soap.

PEGGY: You want a quarter cake a blue soap. Wha happen, miracle happen, de sea open in half. You never wash anyting in yer whole life suddenly you want soap.

MAMA BENIN: (*Turning to go with girls, speaks to* KEN) How come yer bursting so much style terday. Yer didn't sleep hard last night or wat. An you young feller, doh forget tings go start hotting up on de beach bout midday.

(MAMA BENIN *and girls exit.*)

PEGGY: Wha dis going on here. Trow out dat rubbish. (*Throws oyster tulum aside*) Dis is still a rum shop yer 'no. Yer should a wash dem tings from last night.

KEN: A was only passing de time wid customers.

PEGGY: Customers wit no money? You go make a great shop keeper.

KEN: Yer have ter make dem feel at home, den dey go spen money.

PEGGY: Look, just start de washing up. Yer go fine a bucket dey. (*Behind counter; pause*)

(KEN *goes, finds cutlass; picks it up.*)

KEN: Yer 'no, it was a cutlass just like dis a hit im wit.

PEGGY: A hear dat story till I could tell you it backwards.

KEN: How come you doh want ter hear it, an dem girls come all de way round de lagoon ter hear?

PEGGY: All de way wat? Dey fool yer wit dat? All de have ter do is cross it, tide low now, is two minutes an dey home. (*Laughs*) Yer want another joke? I just come back from de post office, an I look in de morning papers; dey had some good news ter day, Mister Ken.

(PEGGY *goes into room.*)

KEN: Murder is a joke? Da is good news?

PEGGY: (*Inside*) Murder wat?

KEN: A dead ole man?

PEGGY: (*Enters*) Notting like dat, but dere was a story bout a feller getting hang, yer 'no dat must be de worst way ter dead, yer tongue hanging out, yer neck twist one side an especially if yer kill yer fadder is no mercy, because de hang man is a fadder too, so he go make de knot extra tight, an de grave digger is a fadder too an he go make de coffin extra narrow, so dey have ter lay yer sideways an yer 'no how uncomfortable dat is, an de noise wen he shovel de earth in? He go do it extra hard, yer go tink yer reach hell already.

KEN: Oh God, Woman, doh keep going on. Only last night you was saying how safe a was, wit all yer here.

PEGGY: A wasn't lying but if you go giving every petticoat dat come in here—an dem who doh ever wear notting underneath—yer story, especially dem two, even de king in England go hear bout it. A sure dat Wilma get it by now an she go....

KEN: Dey go talk?

PEGGY: How long is a river?

KEN: But wat dey go get out of life ter see me hang?

PEGGY: You en 'no. Dey have some funny people in dis world. I 'no a feller used ter eat cockaroach, only cockaroach, a even offer ter give him free food he say no tanks, he like de crunch, so wha it is ter dem ter see you dangling like some granfadder pendulum, an hearing yer neck snap.

KEN: Well, is de lonley stinging nettle track fer me again.

PEGGY: You en go be lonley man. All you have ter do is give dem dat pot hound look an dey go pick you up, you go meet plenty.

KEN: Wat you 'no. You don 'no wat it like ter walk pass a couple in de dark and hear dem breeding an laughing an 'no is not you, or pass a house wit lights on wit children playing an 'no is not yours, or have a dog chase yer ankle an more yer run is de more it chase yer, or smell a pot cooking in de breeze an yer belly bawling wit hunger, you doh 'no.

PEGGY: You is a funny feller yer 'no. One minute yer like one a dem dotish saga boy and de next yer have so much feeling I doh 'no yer.

KEN: Wat funny bout dat? If yer live by yerself yer bound ter grow so.

PEGGY: But I en so, an I live by myself wit me fadder alone.

KEN: How come a nice woman like you could say a ting like dat? I bet all de men in dis village would like ter have you as dere woman, ter get call Playboy Number 1. *I* would.

(PEGGY *goes towards door; looks out, unsettled.*)

PEGGY: Well, I doh 'no wat going on, ter hear you saying dem tings an 'no a nice feller like you have de beast in him ter kill he ole man.

KEN: I doh 'no either, only dat I feel a closeness wit you terday I never feel wit anybody, man, woman, or dog. An watever happen, dat go stay in my heart like a brand, an de further I go from you go make no difference. As far as I concern de only crime I commit is not to have shown you wat a nice person I is, an how good it would be de two a we waking up in de morning greeting de sun wit hope in we hearts, a was going ter say. I'll take me tings an go now, but I en have notting ter take, so I'll take me farewell of you. If I a stay round her a go only get hang. *(Turns to go)*

PEGGY: *(Calling out)* Ken, come back here! So, yer does walk out on a job? Yer is bottle boy here an I en having you skylarking on de job, yer hear!

KEN: But yer say I go get catch if a stay.

PEGGY: I took de trouble an I went down an read all de back papers from last week, an not one a dey had anyting bout murder. De en fine de body, so yer safe here.

KEN: So you was only giving me dat ter hole. Wat a woman you is! So a could stay wit you and we go be together all de time?

(STANLEY runs in, carrying a suitcase. He is followed by MAMA BENIN.)

STANLEY: Peggy! Peggy! A taught yer might be interested in knowing dat yer goats get out an running an yer 'no wat go happen if dey hit de beach. It go be curry goat fer everybody.

PEGGY: A better go. *(Exits)*

KEN: I better go too. She go need more dan one hand.

MAMA BENIN: *(Holding him)* She could manage, dey 'no she. If you go de ram go butt yer. Anyway Stanley here have a little matter ter discuss with yer. *(Sits)*

STANLEY: *(Taking something from his pocket)* Yer see dat, yer 'no wat dat is.

KEN: It say here, is a boat ticket ter Venezuela.

STANLEY: Dat right, an is yours. De oil fields a Venezuela looking fer labor. A man could make plenty money dere.

KEN: A hear dat.

STANLEY: An yer en have ter have no certificate or notting. Plenty money ter make. I was going ter go but a have ter keep my eye on me fleet. An look—*(Opens case)* dey say de nights does get a bit chilly down dey out in de bush. I was going ter carry dese clothes. Yer could have dem too. Look. A new flannel shirt! Brand new! Take it. See if it fit! It bound ter fit. We is de same size. Take it ner. Take de ticket go ner.

(KEN takes the shirt, holds it up to his chest, then stops.)

KEN: So why you want ter get rid a me?

STANLEY: Wat? I en want ter get rid a you. A tell yer I woulda go meself, Venezuela opening up! A young man could make he name.

KEN: I tink you want me outa de way. Ter give you a clear field.

STANLEY: Look, a go tell yer straight pardner. I is a business man. I en no how ter twist people. So is like dis: I an Peggy getting married an I car have a feller like you. I en have notting against you, but it doh look right a brave doh care feller like you living here. People giving me joke already.

KEN: So you go bribe me to go wit a flannel shirt, eh?

STANLEY: Do' get vex ner man. Put yerself in my place. Mama Benin tell him ner.

MAMA BENIN: *(Going over)* Wat Stanley saying is true. You could land down dey wit notten in yer pocket an leave a big shot. An dem Spanish girls love Trinidad Creole man.

STANLEY: Take my word for it. It en go work out. A young fearless feller like you an a young fearless woman like she. All yer go be like cat an dog from de time all yer get up. Fighting and scratching! And dat is only in de morning! What go happen in de evening wen de sun go down? Well is den she go start up. No peace, no peace on Earth, fer you! Is a quiet, tame feller, like me go suit she. If she say boo, I go run. Is all ter do wit yer nature.

MAMA BENIN: Well try on de flannel shirt ner, at least. De man tote de bag all dis way. Wen yer hole it up ter yer de red suit yer, yer 'no. An de blue duck pants, try dem on. *(Pushing him to back room)* Yer doh have ter say yes or no right now. Wear dem ter de regatta, den give we yer answer.

KEN: Alright den. I'd like her ter see me in some nice clothes. *(Exits)*

STANLEY: Yer hear dat. He want her ter see 'im in dem. He en going no way now. I en tink dis was such a good idea after all. Dat man make up he mind to capture Peggy. Wha a go do now? A taught bout writing ter de police bout him, but he go 'no is me an bust outa jail an get me too. If I wasn't such a respectable business man, a would wait fer him one dark night an—but yer 'no.

MAMA BENIN: Yes, dat take a lot a gumption.

STANLEY: Life really hard yer 'no wen yer en have a fadder, yer could easily kill him an everybody go hail yer. Mama Benin yer have ter help me out. All dem dead bat and funny ting yer does burn, yer mean yer can't come up wit someting. A give yer house, rent free for this year.

MAMA BENIN: Rent free, we in August.

STANLEY: August ter August den.

MAMA BENIN: Well, dem is powerful forces you want me ter interfere wit yer 'no.

STANLEY: Cut some cards or burn candle on he head.

MAMA BENIN: Wha bout if I marry him meself.

STANLEY: Better yet.

MAMA BENIN: Dat would solve all yer problems.

STANLEY: Yes. Yes.

MAMA BENIN: Dat would be worth a house and a fishing boat ter me.

STANLEY: A whole house. Yer want ter kill me or wat?

MAMA BENIN: How you tink she go feel if she hear you turn down de chance a getting she fer a house an a fishing boat.

STANLEY: Turn down? I en turn down notting. A bargaining da is all. All good business man does do dat.

MAMA BENIN: A see. Well I is just a simple woman.

STANLEY: Le me see, le me see. Wha bout if I en give yer de house, but let yer have it fer no rent till yer dead.

MAMA BENIN: A might have children.

STANLEY: Wait ner, wait ner. An everyday a drop off two fresh fish on yer. An I buy all de rum an food fer de wedding.

MAMA BENIN: Wha bout de dress, de ring, an de suit an wristwatch fer him?

STANLEY: It cheaper if a marry you miself. Nar, nar. Da is a joke. Yes, yes, alright dem tings too, wha bout dat.

MAMA BENIN: Dat go do.

STANLEY: I 'no you could do it. I hear so much stories bout you, some a dem bound ter be true.

MAMA BENIN: Wha bout me charms an beauty as a woman? Yer doh tink da is enough?

STANLEY: Of course. Of course.

MAMA BENIN: Alright, doh sin yer soul, he coming out now.

(KEN *comes out whistling. He is wearing his new clothes.*)

MAMA BENIN: I say, yer look so good in dem clothes dat yer gone ter call on de governor.

KEN: Na, na. Dey suit me, eh.

MAMA BENIN: Ter a T. It go be a shame ter see you walk up de gang plank ter de mainland.

KEN: Wat gang plank? I en going nowhere. Dis place mighten be much, but I go take it here.

(MAMA BENIN *makes a sign to* STANLEY *to go.*)

STANLEY: Well, a glad yer like de garments, but I have ter go an see wat de tide doing. (*Exits*)

MAMA BENIN: A wasn't lying yer 'no, boy. Dem clothes really suit yer.

KEN: (*In front of mirror*) A 'no. A 'no.

MAMA BENIN: Even King Farouk have ter step aside if he see you coming.

KEN: Yer tink so?

MAMA BENIN: Yes man. Yer en tied a admire yeself. Sit down ner le we talk.

KEN: Nar, no time. A have ter go an see if Peg's need a hand. Oh Lord, it car be no—

MAMA BENIN: (*Going over*) What wrong?

KEN: *(At door)* I—a jumbie, a walking jumbie a me dead fadder.

MAMA BENIN: *(Looking out)* Who, dat ole beggar?

KEN: Yes, a have ter hide. Quick, where?

(The door opens. KEN hides behind it. KEN's father MAC enters.)

MAMA BENIN: Good day ter you ole feller.

MAC: Yer see a young feller pass dis way dis morning or lass night.

MAMA BENIN: You is a beast or wat ter walk in an en even say howdy. Wha kinda manners yer have.

MAC: Yer see im.

MAMA BENIN: Wha he look like.

MAC: Ugly, yes ugly. Wit a look on he face like he tief yer last cent. A feller down de road say he see im coming dis way last night.

MAMA BENIN: Ter day is Discovery Day. A lot a young fellers come here fer de fete. Wat yer want him fer.

MAC: A want ter wipe im off de face of dis Earth fer giving me dis. *(Takes off his hat; his head is bandaged)* He do it, wit a dull cutlass blade. But he en 'no me. I is a bull. Is all week I tracking im with blood pouring out me head an only sucking cane for nourishment.

(MAMA BENIN takes his head in her hands to examine the wound.)

MAMA BENIN: Yer is a bull alright. Dat is a chop an a half. Who do it, a wajank?

MAC: Me own flesh an blood. Me son, me own son do it. He en no wajank or notting. Just a dry dottish excuse for a man.

MAMA BENIN: Yer better watch out fer blood poison, I tink de call it, wit dem flies playing mas on yer head in dis hot sun. Is a hell of a chop he give yer day, yer musta really get 'im vex ter make im chop he own fadder.

MAC: He do it.

MAMA BENIN: Yes, I 'no wat it like wen ole people give young people a hard time.

MAC: Hard? I give dat boy de benefit a my years, care an provide fer him so dat he go look after me wen I get ole, an now look at me, chasing him all over de place.

MAMA BENIN: No rest fer de wicked, eh.

MAC: Who wicked is he! Is he who chop me! Is he who I have ter kick ter get up in morning ter work. An wen he get in de fields, soon as a turn me back, he under some tree sleeping, with he rake an hoe pack up.

MAMA BENIN: He didn't work?

MAC: Work wat? A had ter watch im like a hawk. He take a whole day ter lif up a bundle a cane. A tell im dig a drain, he dig a canal. A tell 'im dig a canal, he dig a drain. If he wasn't doing dat, he was looking in some mirror combing he grass.

MAMA BENIN: Well he musta been a good-looking fellow, going after de women an dem, eh?

MAC: Woman wat? If he see a piece a leg coming cross de field he'd run hide in de ole shed and peep out behind de door like a she cow! Woman wat?

MAMA BENIN: Is de rum dat get im den? Went ter he head?

MAC: Rum he? He smell de cork he would get drunk, an me a heavy rum drinker have he for a son! A tell yer once I give him a puff from a tobacco leaf an had ter put him on my back an carry him home! De ungrateful wretch.

MAMA BENIN: Well, I hear bout some Mama pools in my life, but not one like dat.

MAC: A 'no, yer never! He take de belt! All de girls used ter laugh an pappyshow im, wen dey didn't have no joke on de corner, de used ter come in de field ter get it, ter see im trample an fall down, on he backside wen he see dem coming, dey used ter call im Twirly and Twisty.

MAMA BENIN: A wish a could been dey ter see dat. Yer say he was short like grass.

MAC: Tall like the weeds.

MAMA BENIN: An dark?

MAC: Like de ace a spades, an dirty.

MAMA BENIN: A tink a see a feller like dat yer 'no.

MAC: An ugly ter go wit it.

MAMA BENIN: Yes, an he resemble you.

MAC: Which way he go?

MAMA BENIN: A tink a hear im ask somebody whey ter catch de bus ter Rio Claro, an dey point him right.

MAC: Wen dis was? Yer tink a could haul im back?

MAMA BENIN: If yer take de short cut.

MAC: Whey is dat?

MAMA BENIN: If yer go through Mister Edwards coconut an follow de Dee in de bend, yer go over haul 'im coming round by St. Andrews, den sit down an wait fer im by Number 43 Mile Post.

MAC: A taught you say it was a short cut.

MAMA BENIN: Da is it. Is either dat or he gone forever.

MAC: Alright den. (Exits)

MAMA BENIN: *(Calling out)* A hope yer catch him an twice give im good, wat he have coming ter him. But spare he life, because he sound like he en worth swinging fer. Remember vengence is mine said de Lord. *(She closes the door and laughs at* KEN.*)* So you is de living, breeding Playboy a de West Indies.

*(*KEN *opens the door a little. Checks to see that* MAC *is gone.)*

KEN: Mama Benin wha a go do? Wat Peggy go tink wen she get dat story? What she go say?

MAMA BENIN: So it's Peggy now! A minute ago it was Pegs!

KEN: Mama Benin, you have to help me! What a go do?

MAMA BENIN: Yer go do wat I do, last, wen I get rid a my old man. I catch myself walking in de forest picking up beetles and pieces a wood, or walking on de beach, a dead fish or pink crab shell an all de times seeing de big ships going, never coming an knowing everyone was taking young, strong handsome fellers away from me, and I go live longer and longer by myself. But I have me house, an because we on a hill is dere de old men come ter sit an smoke. An dere you will hear stories round de coppra fire dat will fill yer head wit magic and wisdom, dat will last yer two lifetimes an make yer feel yer read every book in de world, an after dey gone and de night chill hit we, we would go an rub up an hug up an....

ALICE: *(Outside, calling)* Ken, big Ken, come ner.

KEN: Is Peggy.

IVY: *(Outside, calling)* Hot boy Ken. Whey yer.

MAMA BENIN: Nar, is dem two lil girls, come ter carry yer ter de fete. Wat yer want me ter tell dem.

KEN: Help me ter get Peggy back. You must 'no how it is ter ache an pain fer somebody.

ALICE: *(Nearer)* Le me see yer ner. Yer fraid we eat yer?

MAMA BENIN: If I help yer wha yer go do fer me, besides smile a grateful smile every time a pass yer. Yer would buy me house for me, dis place does turn a good raise, an wen yer get make official man here.

IVY: Yer playing hard ter get or wat?

KEN: Yes, yes, a kiss de cross. *(He crosses both forefingers and kisses X.)*

MAMA BENIN: Alright den. Dat ole feller was never here. So yer see, yer safe, Peggy en go 'no a ting till she dead.

KEN: Supposing he come back.

MAMA BENIN: I go say he's a madman from way back come ter look fer he son who wash overboard or someting.

(ALICE and IVY enter.)

IVY: Come ner man. Everybody down on de beach. Peggy send we fer yer.

ALICE: De small boat start ter race already an we put aside a big one fer you.

IVY: An some fellers playing some sweet music.

ALICE: Come ner man.

KEN: A go come if Peggy dey.

IVY: She cooking a goat an mamaguying poor Stanley.

KEN: A comin. *(They start to exit.)*

ALICE: It call Santa Maria de Tird.

KEN: De goat.

IVY: No, de boat, chupid.

(All laugh as they exit. MAMA BENIN stays.)

MAMA BENIN: Well, if de worst come ter de worst, it go be really funny ter see if all he have ter fall back on is me, a obeah woman who bury she children an get rid a she ole man. *(After a beat she exits.)*

CURTAIN

ACT THREE

(Scene: The rum shop. Late afternoon. JIM *enters, a little drunk.)*

JIM: *(Calls out)* Peggy? Anybody home?

*(*PHIL *enters, in the same state.)*

JIM: Yer see her?

PHIL: No. It's Mikey we want. A sen Stanley wit de wheel barrow to get im, I see him run drunk, but never one as bad as dat. An she is anoder one, locking away all de good rum. A man could die a thirst round here, she so busy running after dat new feller.

JIM: Yer can blame she. He bust de over an under lucky seven man! An trow de only hoop ter go round de doll, an dat en all! He eat ten doubles an twelve sweet drink, an he enter fer de tug 'a war, de greasy pole, an de big boat race, an I leave im dancing wit two women. Dat man born lucky.

PHIL: Luck or not, he better watch out. He can't open he mouth ter yawn witout bragging how he chop he ole man an how de blade flashing in de sun an....

*(*PHIL *brings bottle and glasses.)*

JIM: Yer find some.

PHIL: Bound to. Yer 'no me. Horse ter water. Le we kill it ner.

JIM: A man can't hang by informing on himself, an he fadder rot by now, crapeaux smoke he pipe.

PHIL: But suppose, just suppose somebody go digging ditch right were he put de body, de right spot! It does happen yer 'no, an a jawbone come up followed by a piece a han wit fingers, wat dey go say in de police headquarters. Just suppose.

JIM: Suppose your nose was a door post hose. You doh 'no dem, man! Dem professor an ting go say it was some Carib or Awarak king, or one a Columbus boys get left behind. I hear dey have plenty bones in de Institute, wit piece a jug an plate.

(MAC *enters and sits by door.*)

PHIL: You believe dat?

JIM: Why not, you feel Mama Benin is de only obeah woman in de world.

PHIL: No. Dey have plenty.

JIM: Dem professors an ting does take out bones an put dem together an fine out which horse go win wat race.

PHIL: I hear if yer grind up bones and drink it, yer totie stan up all night. It give yer real strength.

MAC: (*Getting up;* PHIL *and* JIM *turn.*) I never drink no bones, but I stronger dan both a all yer. Look at dat. (*Showing them his wound*) All yer tink all yer could walk round wit a chop like dat from a cutlass, a sharp cutlass.

(PHIL *and* JIM *cautiously approach and examine head.*)

PHIL: Lord, who chop yer man?

MAC: Me own son chop me! Yer could believe dat? Me own son a tell yer!

JIM: Well yer live an learn.

PHIL: How he do it, Pardner?

MAC: Give me a eights en a go tell yer. Yer 'no how much road I walk, getting place ter sleep an food ter eat, just fer telling people de true story?

(MAMA BENIN *appears at the door.*)

(PHIL *goes for glass.*)

PHIL: Mama Benin come in ner an hear dis.

MAMA BENIN: *(To* MAC*)* Is you agin. Wha happen, yer catch cramp? After I go ter all de trouble ter give you de right directions?

MAC: I see de bus man. I see de bus take off, an me troat feel a bit dry an yer right, a catch a cramp in dis one, no it was dis one.

MAMA BENIN: Yer sure it wasn't in yer mouth.

MAC: Nar, Man, dat alright, so a say ter meself le 'im go long, wit de Devil for company, an a turn back.

(MAMA BENIN *pours another drink for* MAC.*)*

MAMA BENIN: Yer right. Rest yer weary bones, an fire another one. Yer must be dead out tramping round de bush. *(She drinks from bottle.)* One fer de road. *(They drink.)*

MAC: *(Goes to look around)* Tank yer. Dey is a nice place all yer have here man.

MAMA BENIN: *(To men)* All yer 'no who dat is.

MEN: No.

MAMA BENIN: He's a mad man who bang he own head on de mile post. I meet im dis morning telling people he doh like mile post, dey is de wrong shape. Yer could beat dat.

PHIL: Wat shape he want dem ter be?

MAMA BENIN: Shut up an listen ner, before he come back. He hear de story bout de young feller, wat he name, Ken. Yes, Ken. He hear bout Ken, so yer 'no wha, he say Ken is he son an Ken chop im. Yer ever hear madness like dat? Dat en no joke madness yer 'no! Dat is true, true madness! An saying he go kill 'im fer chopping he head.

PHIL: He "gone." He see Ken yet?

MAMA BENIN: No, an you doh mention notting 'bout 'im or else you go be witness if any killing go on. All yer doh say notting. I go Mama guy 'im an we go see how mad he really is, an all yer go see how lucky yer is not ter be made like dat.

JIM: Yes.

PHIL: Dere but fer de grace a God go us, eh.

MAMA BENIN: (Loud) So how yer feeling now old feller? De rum strengthen yer? Yer like de place?

MAC: Yes, a was saying ter meself how nice it is.

MAMA BENIN: Yer does talk ter yer self a lot den. I does do it too.

MAC: Yes. I en feeling so bad, now, tank God, considering de way a is. Wen I tinka how I look after dat boy, from de minute he born, help im wit he home work, he was a real dunce yer no, didn't even no wat one an one was.

JIM: Two.

PHIL: Facts, facts.

(During the course of this speech MAMA BENIN is smiling at PHIL and JIM, sneering at MAC.)

MAMA BENIN: Ter hear you talking so quiet, nobody would believe you was de same feller who pass terday, yer sure.

MAC: Is me a tell yer, who yer tink a is? Is me, ole man who see life come an go, who see hunger an poverty an en want ter see it again. An ter have yer only hope in life go ter de dogs, yer pride an joy, and after you spend yer hole life saving up yer blessing fer 'im.

PHIL: *(To* JIM) He mad? He en mad! *(To* MAMA BENIN) Ask 'im wat he son was like.

MAMA BENIN: Dis son a yours, de one dat hit yer, he was handsome an good at high jump an long jump, beating everybody?

MAC: Yer en hear me say he was bazódee? He didn't 'no he left foot from he right.

MAMA BENIN: Fire another, ner.

MAC: Tanks. *(Takes bottle, pours)*

MAMA BENIN: *(To* PHIL *and* JIM) Is de rum talking.

(A cheer comes from outside.)

MAC: Wha is all dat noise for?

MAMA BENIN: Dey rating up a young feller, de champion Playboy of de West Indies.

(Another cheer)

MAC: *(At window)* Is race dey racing.

JIM: *(At door)* Yes man, yer can't see de boats, dey go race from dey ter de point den back, dat's de playboy in de red, white, an blue one.

MAC: A could see dem. Dey coming round from de point. Who's dat? Who's dat leading? A can't see too good.

MAMA BENIN: Yes, a blow ter de head does change yer eyes.

MAC: Dat one, yer say? If you tell me he was a dope a would say he favor me killer son plenty.

MAMA BENIN: Dat's de saga boy a tell yer, an everyting he touch terday turn ter gold.

PHIL: Look dey catching up wit 'im, dey closing de gap.

JIM: He go win, he go win.

PHIL: Not yet Jim, too soon ter talk, yer go put goat mout on 'im.

MAMA BENIN: Watch 'im bend dat back, look at dem arms move, dat is rowing fer so.

MAC: Dat boat cutting de water.

MAMA BENIN: A wave hit him cross side, he lose he rhythm, he drop a oar, nar he catch it wid one hand, an coming back again.

PHIL: He passing two.

MAMA BENIN: A tell yer.

JIM: He pass anodder. One more to go.

MAMA BENIN: He go do it, he go do it.

PHIL: We go see.

JIM: Is neck an neck.

MAC: *(Shouts)* De odder feller driving im ter de beach, he en go have room ter pass.

MAMA BENIN: He go do it, he go do it.

JIM: Dey still neck an neck.

MAC: He go do it now, now, now, he do it. *(Cheers from beach)* Wat dey doing, wat dey doing, is dat rum dey give im ter drink, an look dey putting flowers round he head, well I—dey coming up—is Ken, so help me God, a no de way he wipe he nose on he hand an he is a hero?

(He jumps down and runs. MAMA BENIN catches him and pulls him back.)

MAMA BENIN: Stay here man, dat en yer son. *(To* JIM*)* Hold 'im.

JIM: A go hole 'im, a go hole 'im.

MAC: Le me go. Let me go. A go kill 'im! A go dance on he blood terday!

MAMA BENIN: Dat en yer son a tell yer, dat feller going ter marry de daughter a dis rum shop, which make plenty money an it have a license, an more punch en rum dat you could drink in two life time. Yer sure da is yer son?

MAC: He marrying she?

MAMA BENIN: Yes, dat one dey cheering.

MAC: A decent-looking girl like dat, an she have a raise? Yer lie! Yer must be crazy. Dis is a mad house a in, a 'no one day if a carry on....

MAMA BENIN: Is you mad, dat chop on yer head sen yer, dat feller is de King a de West Indies.

MAC: But is Ken a tell yer.

(Cheers outside)

MAMA BENIN: Da is ter tell you, yer mad, yer en hear how dey rating 'im coming up de hill, an you say yer son is a dope. Dey wouldn't be cheering 'im, dat sound like a dope dey cheering?

MAC: A 'no, it doh make no sense at all. *(Cheers)* I really going mad now yer 'no. (MAC *sits, head in hands.)* I see some tings in my life yer 'no. One time I see a soukingya flying through de night in a ball a fire after sucking somebody blood, an in de morning a had a bruise on me neck. Anodder time a walking home one night an a hear chains dragging behind me, wen a look back a see dis shrivel-up old woman wit light in she eyes, an is a good ting a light a cigarette, because she turn back saying, yer lucky, yer lucky. But I never taught de day would come wen I would mistake dat idiot for a heffea. A really gone now.

MAMA BENIN: I really not suprise, wit yer brain open ter de sun and rain beating down on it.

MAC: Is blight. A blight! Dat is all! I never feel so mash up, like dis. I run hores fer a week wen we had dat big harvest in '32, fer a whole week, an I bounce back. But dis. You sound like a wise woman, me mind gone. Yer tink a bush bath could help put me back?

MAMA BENIN: It gone too far. I 'no bout cures but I never see a case as bad as dis. Yer en hear yer.

MAC: *(Getting up, forced cheerful)* Well. A better be going den. Dey have people who go be glad ter see me yer 'no. *(Boasting)* An I, de state a in, had a teacher feller writing down everyting a say fer he history book, yer'd never believe dat en, looking at me, a real teacher with papers ter he name an ting.

MAMA BENIN: Wonders never cease.

MAC: Dey sent ter try us.

MAMA BENIN: Well, if yer going, yer better go quick yer 'no. Because de last madman de catch in dis village dey pelt 'im an souk de dogs an 'im, till he end up in a ball crying an wailing, den dey put 'im in a bag an drop im off de point.

MAC: Yes. Yes, is wen yer mad, yer does see wat human beings made outa. A go duck out de side an miss dem.

MAMA BENIN: *(Showing him out)* Yes. If yer hog de side a de shed an make fer de young coconut, nobody go see you.

MAC: A gone. *(He goes off.)*

PHIL: Yer flying some kinda kite Mama Benin, but I go catch up with 'im an give 'im some food an a bit ter rest, and a go see who mad, you or me!

MAMA BENIN: Go. Go ner, but, a warning yer, watchout fer yer own head, yer en hear 'im talk bout de crazy tings he do.

PHIL: I go watch out, but you watch out too, because someting tell me we go see some baccanal before ternight over.

(PHIL *goes,* JIM *goes laughing.*)

(*Voices*)

ALICE: An wen de oar fall out yer hand a taught yer really had it an den yer just catch it so.

IVY: I too, I too.

(KEN *enters with shirt tied around waist, with* PEGGY, ALICE, *and* IVY.)

PEGGY: Alright all yer, tanks fer seeing us here, but de poor boy wear out now an he pouring wit sweat, so all yer give 'im a break.

ALICE: Yer doh want 'im too tired, eh.

IVY: Not wid he blood so close ter he skin.

PEGGY: Look, all yer go an see de tug-a-war, all dem big fellers straining an sweating in de tight bathing trunks.

ALICE: Alright Peggy, but hold he prizes, de silver cup donated by Stanley, a new white shirt an a pair a serge trousers.

(PEGGY *takes things.*)

KEN: (*Kissing girls*) Tanks, de both a all yer, fer carrying me trophies an keeping me company de way up here, but if you tink ter day I was some ting, yer shoulda see me de day a chop me fadder head.

VOICE: (*Outside, male:*) All yer come, de tug-a-war starting now.

PEGGY: Yes, all yer go, or else yer go miss it. Let 'im ress an dry off, he can't do no more terday.

(PEGGY *ushers girls out.*)

MAMA BENIN: Yes, come girls. Peggy have she own, le we see wat de tide bring in fer we.

(*They go out.* PEGGY *wipes* KEN's *shoulders, chest with cloth.*)

PEGGY: Well, a hope yer pleased wit yer self an so yer should be, after all yer beat dem coming an going. Nobody en even come close, even de greasy pole yer mount dat like a bull. From now on yer could win anyting. An yer sweating so. (*Passes her fingers on his chest and tastes*) Em. It salty an nice.

KEN: Winning dese en go be notting compared ter de king prize I after, an dat is yer promise yer go marry me in two weeks time.

PEGGY: You real bold face ter ask me dat, wen we 'no yer going back ter de girl in your village, once yer ole man turn carcuss.

KEN: Going whey? Wat girl? Not me! I en going no whey. I en have nobody ter go back to, a tell yer. Is just you an me. De rainy season comin an we go just lie in bed an listen ter it beating on de galvanise roof an feel cosy like two small children. An at night we go stan by de door an smell de hibiscus circling in de breeze an count de stars an miscount an start over again. Wha yer say?

PEGGY: An if we loving so all de time, who go run de shop? You en go have no strength left ter do notting else!

KEN: No strength left? Yer en see wha happen ter day, I was a Samson, an dat was a taste. I go do both, love you like a baby *an* run tings.

PEGGY: Yer so sure.

KEN: Yer go see. My love go give you strength, and yours go give me more strength, and yer go see de shop go run itself.

PEGGY: Dat would be really someting ter see. Whey you learn ter rhapsody so?

KEN: You en hear notting yet. Yer go see wen we go ter Toco on Good Friday and we drink some chip chip soup an we wash it down with coconut water, a go pass de jelley ter yer wit a wet kiss an wen yer strech on de sand a go pour some sweet oil on yer an sooth yer till yer sleep.

PEGGY: A might en want ter sleep.

KEN: We go do de next best ting den.

PEGGY: Wha is dat?

KEN: Dats. (PEGGY *puts hands on* KEN's *lips.*)

PEGGY: It should be nice.

KEN: More dan nice. If you 'no de power you bring out in me, I never had before.

PEGGY: I feel it.

KEN: I fraid ter talk bout it, dat some millionaire might hear an come an take you away, man who have everyting but dat power. Money, pretty pictures, house, big car, but dey 'no someting en dere, dat all de money in London can't buy. It have ter be given freely an wit out contract.

PEGGY: An wat it is wid me, dat bring out all dis in you, dat make me tink a listening ter de sea foaming at night an a bird singing?

KEN: You! Is you! I was walking, no *stumbling*, in de dark, fer ages cutting me foot, kicking stones, an den I see dis light soon as a walk in dis shop, dere was a light dat brighten de way an a saw every obstacle ter pass.

PEGGY: If a was yer wife, dat light would go wherever you go, brighten every whey, an I en such a bad cook either an a could mend an sew.

KEN: Dat a 'no.

PEGGY: A could also play tic-tac-toe wid stones skimming de waves, an give yer a horse back.

KEN: Too risky, too risky, yer might sprain yer shoulders or put yer back out. No, none a dat, just....

PEGGY: We could share a baby cot an make it have room for more—but dis could be just ole talk. I doh 'no you might get tired staying in a dry rum shop and notting ter amuse a bright penny like you.

KEN: (*Embraces her*) If a didn't already sin me soul, a woulda put me hand in fire an swear to eat grass an stones, dat what I say is true.

PEGGY: Dat good den, because I don 'no who ter tank, de road, de stars, de moon, or de sun, or all a dem because one a dem or someting bring you to me an a no a lucky fer dat day. An a have de hanbag, shoes, and dress already, so we can get married wen we like. I can't believe is me doing dis Ken. Everybody 'no my mouth like a cat 'o nine tails even when I make a joke, it used ter cut people up, an now dis! Wen mango ripe it go really fall, because from dis day en no couple in Mayaro can touch we, for love an devotion.

(*Drunken singing is coming from outside.*)

Song: Rum, glorious rum,
Wen a call yer yer bound ter come,
Yer was made a Caroni cane,
An brewed in Port of Spain
A going ter bring me scorpion ter

Bite yer Santapiede
San-e-man-e-teh.

(MIKEY *enters, being pushed in a wheel barrow by* STANLEY.
MIKEY *sings inside.)*

STANLEY: *(To* PEGGY*)* Look yer fadder. We had ter take
de long way. Too much people would see im an get de
wrong impression.

PEGGY: Wat is dat?

(During this, MIKEY *is attempting to get out.)*

STANLEY: Well, am, you 'no....

PEGGY: *(Laughs)* Poor Stanley, never mind everbody 'no
'im.

*(*MIKEY *gets out, goes to* KEN.*)*

MIKEY: Greetings, an hail to you young feller. I hear yer
bust everybody ass down dey. Dey still reeling, a really
sorry a miss de ole baccaal man, but de wake was just
as good. If yer see woman just wait fer de eye, an some
a dem en even waiting! Dey giving it! A good-looking
feller like you woulda rake dem in like pebbles! Wen de
time come ter drop him in de hole, is only Nancy man
was left holding hand, all de odders was in de bush,
some whey, brushing woman. Is a good ting Fred was a
lightweight.

KEN: It sound good.

MIKEY: Yes man, a tell yer, an you is a hell of a feller
man, trowing yer poor old man in some ditch instead a
giving 'im a good send-off wid a wake where all he pals
could gather round he body an tell tales of de deeds an
scrapes he get up ter, instead a...wha happen, yer too
cheap ter buy rum and food or wat? I woulda stan it.

KEN: Dat would a be too good fer 'im.

MIKEY: Listen ter 'im ner. A real desperado, wha is your name, Zorro or Jesse James. Boy de men in dis village go have ter watch you. If you take a shine ter dey women it go be murder. *(Pointing)* But take Stanley der fer instance.

STANLEY: Not me. Not. *(Demurring)*

MIKEY: Shut up Stanley, a praising yer.

STANLEY: Or—

MIKEY: Stanley is a decent, God-fearing, fine, upstanding man wit pedigree an wit a future ahead a him. He going places I en no where. But he go amount ter someting yer no wat a mean. An dat is de man I want fer a son-in-law, an I ask de post mistress ter marry dem ter day.

JIM: More fete!

KEN: Ter day yer say.

MIKEY: An ter day it is. Yer tink I chupid as well as drunk, ter have a tricky feller like you under de same roof as my single daughter? Besides, de time come.

PEGGY: An de post mistress say yes.

MIKEY: Not only, yes. Also,I'd be honored to oblige a neighbor.

PEGGY: Dis was after or before yer carry she in de bush.

KEN: Peg.

MIKEY: You stay outa dis. Yer wipe yer foot.

PEGGY: I wipe it fer him. An he inside de door now because is he an he alone I marrying.

MIKEY: He? Dat feller? You making he my son-in-law? And he hand still damp wit he fadder blood.

PEGGY: I en go end up dry an bitter because I marry dat English gentleman ter please you an Mistress Field. I

want a man wit blood an magic in him ter keep me
warm an alive in old age.

MIKEY: Well you is de most ungrateful daughter I ever
come across.

PEGGY: Why? How much yer come across?

MIKEY: Don't try an change de subject. I 'no yer tricks.
You tink because I drunk yer could get through, but I
catch yer red handed in de act. Dey say a man son is he
pride an he daughter is he joy. Well, you is....Help me
out ner Stanley—yer en jealous? How you could let a
man walk in here an waltz off wit yer woman?

STANLEY: Wha I go do against a man who kill he own
fadder?

PEGGY: Well is a good ting is not you I choose or else I
left ter fen fer me own self in dis wicked world. Praise
God. He keep me occupied till Ken come in off de road.

STANLEY: Yer didn't have ter go grabbing de first Tom,
Dick, or Harry vagabond dat....

PEGGY: A suppose life wid you woulda been purely
governor balls an fancy masquerades with fire work
popping at midnight. Nar, it woulda been wipe de
mayor backside because he have pull. Or help Wilma
gut de carite, not me.

STANLEY: You know what you ain't do? Yer en take into
account my hot feeling fer you. An wat it go mean fer
we two families coming together! We could own dis
village! De two life blood rum an fish, we have right
here in we hand.

PEGGY: I en want ter own no village, Stanley. I want ter
live here, nar, you too decent an ambitious. I go get my
wonder from seeing green mango turn red as if de
breeze rub rouge on dey cheeks. You want some high-
bred mulatto woman who could play parlor games an

ride side ways an give yer horns wit yer best friend, an dat go be "out're". So go' long, good time wasting fer you. *(Goes to* KEN)

STANLEY: Yer en hear me say....

KEN: Ease we man, yer en hear? Or you want ter end up another trophy?

MIKEY: Kill im, is kill yer go kill im too? Is blood yer like spill? Well yer en go do it in my place. Nobody en go come in my place ter enjoy a drink an have murder in front a dem. If is fight all yer want ter fight, go down on de beach.

(MIKEY *pushes* STANLEY *toward* KEN.)

STANLEY: Nar, nar. I en go fight him. I en no Bad John! I radder stay on my own, wit me true feelings in me heart dan tangle wit a beast like him! You fight him, Mikey. Is your daughter he bamboozle an stop us from sharing de spoils of a fleet a three twelve-foot pirogues and dozens a thirsty coppra cutters an fisherman.

JIM: Facts, facts.

STANLEY: You fight him!

MIKEY: Me, fight him. Yer en hear he pass he exam in fadder killing, an yer telling me....You fight him. Fight him now, a backing yer, use de right, de right.

(STANLEY *moves forward a little.*)

STANLEY: Me right hand?

JIM: Heave.

MIKEY: Den de left.

STANLEY: Hand?

MIKEY: No, foot, man. Kick him in de chest den give 'im de coconut head first.

STANLEY: He too tall.

JIM: Now real fight start!

MIKEY: Wait, wait. (*Cuts cutlass and gives to* STANLEY)
Here, chop 'im wid dis. He 'fraid cutlass, he 'no wat
damage it could do.

STANLEY: If a kill 'im dey go hang me man.

JIM: More wake to come!

(STANLEY *puts cutlass down,* KEN *picks it up.*)

KEN: Well, make up yer mind. Is either you or me, wit
we toes up, in hang man cemetry. (STANLEY *runs out.*)
Well, good riddance is wat I say, because you didn't
really want a feller who frighten a he own shadow
round yer. Why yer doh say yer happy fer me an make
she feel good, because my knock's in, an whey ever I go
I go meet good fortune. So catch while catch can.

PEGGY: Yer better do it, cause do it or not I marrying
him so help me God.

(MIKEY *gets up, holds the two of them together.*)

MIKEY: Wha a go do? I can't fight de sea an de sky. If
bad go come of it or good come of it, is outa my hands.
Is a natural ting dat happen ter all yer, wit no contract
or dowry an da is the way tings should happen. Is also
natural fer man ter want ter breed an have he name go
on till it pass de horizon. A man alone on de road
bouncing he toes, wearing out shoe leather, only profit
de shoe maker. No, a wife, a solid roof fer wen de sea
blow, an children running round he yard, dats wat a
man need. Plenty people would tink twice a inviting a
feller like you into he family because dey wouldn't 'no
whey ter expect de next chop from, but I live good an a
go dead good, an a radder dead with plenty healthy
grandchildren crying, dan some sickly minge dat
Stanley would a give me, a man with back bone is a
man ter treasure an you who chop up yer fadder wit

one blow have back bone fer all a we an some left over, so a happy fer all yer so go forward and multiply.

(PEGGY kisses him.)

PEGGY: Amen.

KEN: Amen.

(There is shouting outside. MAC runs in with stick—piece of oar—followed by JIM, PHIL, STANLEY, MAMA BENIN, and IVY and ALICE. MAC goes for KEN, pushes him over, and kicks and punches him. PEGGY grabs MAC's arm.)

PEGGY: Yer mad or wat? Stop dat. Who is you?

MAC: I is he fadder, a shame ter say.

PEGGY: More shame on yer. He fadder dead.

MAC: *(Holding off)* You tink all it take is a dull cutlass blade, rested on yer head?

PEGGY: *(To KEN)* So is a lie. A lie yer tell, saying you downed him. Wat else was a lie, eh?

KEN: He en my fadder, he's a mad man who go bout threatening people. My fadder is a—ask she. She 'no he dead. *(To MAMA BENIN)*

PEGGY: An you is de feller we praise an rate up ter high Heaven, an yer en do notting but tap him an take off wit yer heart in yer mout! Go way from here!

KEN: So wha bout all de feats I do ter day? Wat dey count for eh? Yer see wat a could do, wat heights me could reach? Breaks me from de ole man, an a go show yer more, why yer want me ter end up a wreck now?

PEGGY: Is yer lies an decite dat yer getting back. Wen I tink just half hour ago I was ready ter hitch my sail ter your mast, a shake. *(To MAC)* Take him, take 'im from here before people see me shaking fer a slave owner spy, an a fool of fools to boot. I en 'no what possess me.

PHIL: Take 'im old man. Whose de king a Mayaro now?

MAC: (To KEN) Yer ready? Is licks like peas fer you, an wen a done beat yer, a go beat yer again. Come an take yer lick like a man. (Going towards KEN)

JIM: I backin' de winner.

KEN: (Backing off) Wha you have wit me man? A leave yer on de ground, dat wasn't enough. A didn't want yer by me, yer follow me all de way here. Leave me alone ner man. I never mean you no harm except dat one time.

MAC: Yer begging! Doh beg man. Big man who piss an froth on wall doh beg. No harm, is people like you who doh mean no harm does do de most! Come.

KEN: Mama Benin, tell him.

MAMA BENIN: I try me best all morning. Is between you an he now.

KEN: (To crowd) Alright. All yer satisfied? All yer get de excitement? All yer was looking for? All yer en satisfied a man come among all yer an give life, interest, an daring, dat yer children go be please ter hear about. No, yer have ter seem 'im pull down, too, all in one day, eh? Wat a greedy place is Mayaro.

ALICE: Ask Peggy ter santuary you.

KEN: Nar, cause dat is a woman wit plenty love in she dat is pure an natural an de fire dat burn de love, burn de hate an dat's de fire I warmed to, how did I tink I was worthy a putting my hands in dem flames?

PEGGY: Take him nar. Get im out a hear before a get de boys ter do it here.

MAC: Yer coming or yer want an audience ter see yer tail between yer leg.

PEGGY: (Half laughing, half crying) Is de only place fer it. Show im fer wat he really is. Yer tink we in dis village backwards eh? We go believe every roaming louse who come here....

(MAC *grabs* KEN. KEN *pulls away.*)

KEN: Le me go.

JIM: Dat's it Ken, now real fight start.

(*Crowd agrees.*)

MAC: Come here a say. (*Grabs* KEN)

KEN: Le me go, a tell yer.

MAC: Yes a will, after a break yer back an yer eye can't open.

IVY: Take 'im Ken.

JIM: Dis fight go put we on de map. Bust he face.

PHIL: Lock he neck.

KEN: All yer enjoying dis eh, all yer hungry fer blood, ter see man spill he fellow man blood, an dis is de place I taught I could pass me days in peace an tranquility. Is a good ting dis happen ter day. I was yer hero terday because yer believe a lie. Now I is just a game cock wit money on me head. (MAC *goes for* KEN. KEN *evades.*) Back off a tell yer, or else dey go see wat happen in de privacy of a cane field dat dey would pay theater tickets fer.

(KEN *backs into counter where cutlass is, leans over, and picks it up. Crowd scatters as he swings it. During the squaring off and confrontation, STANLEY pretends to ignore it, but drops guard and is involved when KEN is on receiving end.*)

PHIL: (*To crowd*) He mad. All yer run fer all yer life.

KEN: Is I who mad. Well if all yer sane, yes, I proud ter be mad. Yes.

MAC: Shut yer mout an come outside.

KEN: A coming, but I go chop you up.

(KEN *runs at* MAC. MAC *runs out, followed by* KEN. *Crowd, shouting, goes out.*)

CROWD: *(Outside)* Heave, heave.

(*Shouting stops.* KEN *enters, dazed. He sits down, holding blood-stained cutlass.* MAMA BENIN *enters.*)

MAMA BENIN: Dey getting worked up against you. Run man or dey go hang yer fer sure.

KEN: Nar. After dis Peggy go be back in my corner now.

MAMA BENIN: Come ner man, you en no wat dey like. Dey looking fer knife an bull pistle, anyting dey could come ter you wit.

KEN: I en going no wey an leave she behind. It would be de same if dey get me.

MAMA BENIN: Dis island full ter overflowing wit woman like she.

KEN: Is she an she alone a want.

ALICE: *(Running in)* De coming ter get him, Mama Benin. What we do do? Le we put some ole clothes on him an....

(*They get old straw hat, jacket from nails on wall, attempt to dress him.*)

KEN: All yer doh understand wat love, true love is. *(Pulls away)* Le me go. Le me go a tell yer. After ter day she bound ter marry me, because I come through natural, no lie.

MAMA BENIN: Take de right hand, I go do de left. *(She is holding jacket.)* Come.

KEN: *(Pulling away)* Whey yer taking me? Whay she? All yer want we...is jealous all yer jealous da is it, is we wedding all yer doh want eh? *(He picks up cutlass and*

raises it.) All yer doh listen or wat, get de hence away.
I'd chop man, woman, an child fer she.

MAMA BENIN: Well, is de mad house you belong, no lie.
Jail an de rope too good. Le we go an get de post
mistress, she go save him.

*(MAMA BENIN and ALICE go off through inner room. Men
with weapons appear at door. KEN is sitting with back to
door. MIKEY is carring a rope.)*

MIKEY: De ole man dead.

PHIL: I hear 'im groan an he head nod.

MIKEY: Well, if he wasn't dead before, he dead now. De
way he sitting dey we could creep up an trow a
slippery knot over he head.

PHIL: Let Stanley do it, he more steady den we.

STANLEY: Me? Not me. He go single me out fer he
special grudge. You do it, Peggy.

PEGGY: Come ner.

*(PEGGY creeps forward with others—they drop rope over
KEN.)*

KEN: Wha wrong wit yer?

STANLEY: *(As others pull the rope tight over KEN's arms)*
We have yer now. Is de almond tree fer you. Yer neck
pop.

MIKEY: Yes. De Lord go forgive us fer letting dis
happen on he blessed village. You go fine yours in
Heaven, so come quietly a beg yer. Is de best way.

JIM: For all concerned.

PHIL: Yes, no trouble.

JIM: We go bury yer proper.

STANLEY: Hold him tight.

KEN: I en moving, an wat you have ter do wit dis? Yer en have notting ter say ter me after a do dis ting in front every body, eh.

PEGGY: A stranger go always bring mystery an excitement wit him, but deres a difference between talking big bout killing an de nasty bloody ting dat went on out dey. All yer carry him ter de beach an get it over wit, I go say a turn 'im down an he string up heself.

KEN: So is you who go poison me name fer years ter come, after all we....

(MEN *jerk rope.*)

PHIL: Come man.

(KEN *falls on floor and locks his legs around the table.*)

KEN: Take de cutlass an cut de rope Peggy, a beg yer! At least in jail a preacher go pray fer me! A promise never ter set eyes on yer again. If yer no wat dat would mean, a beg yer....

PEGGY: An have de Lord bring down his vengeance on dis village? No rain fer de provision, an empty nets everytime de boats come in? We had dat already one time. All yer take him ner.

STANLEY: Put de rope on he neck an le we drag him down like a dead cow.

PHIL: You do it. We go hold him.

(STANLEY *gets rope with a hanging noose.*)

MIKEY: Make sure he can't touch yer, he might take yer wit him.

STANLEY: I too 'fraid, man. Peggy, get de cutlass. If he move, chop im.

(PEGGY *gets cutlass, stands over* KEN.)

PEGGY: Don't move or a go chop yer twice.

KEN: You go chop me now, eh? Dats wat everybody was trying ter tell me. Alright, but all yer watch out, because if is hang a have ter hang a go do it, but between here an de almond tree a go make sure an take a few a all yer wit me, mark my words.

STANLEY: Hold 'im tight all yer. You do de rope. Peggy, I go take de cutlass. (*They exchange*) All I want is a excuse ter....

KEN: Ter wat, chop me neck?

(KEN *squirms round on floor and bites* STANLEY.)

STANLEY: Oh God, he bite me. Hold 'im ner, a taught all yer holding him.

MIKEY: Is you have de cutlass, chop him ner.

KEN: Dat bite had poison in it, yer treat a man as a dog an dats wat yer get. Yer go dead blabbering an foaming green at de mouth.

STANLEY: Oh, God.

(MAC *staggers in and looks on, unnoticed.*)

PHIL: Slip it on ner.

PEGGY: A have 'im. (*She puts noose over his head.*)

MIKEY: Good girl.

STANLEY: Yes.

KEN: Yer just kill me.

(PEGGY *is holding neck rope; men are holding* KEN's *arms, drag* KEN *to door by rope.* STANLEY *is carrying the cutlass, raised.* JIM *sees* MAC.)

JIM: Oh, God. Look who came in.

(*They let go of rope and back off.*)

(KEN *gets up.*)

KEN: Yer en tired dead, yer want ter again, why yer doh lay down, man?

MAC: Wat dey tie yer up fer?

KEN: Ter hang me down on de beach fer killing you.

MIKEY: Is natural fer people ter want ter protect dey village an family. Wat would a happen if we let a killer loose, wandering free, wit men in fear an women in wonder?

MAC: (*Untying* KEN) I en care bout yer women. Every peacock have ter look after he own pea hen. An as fer yer men I en see one here I'd call dat. Barring two, an dem two go be leaving now, fer de fresh air an freedom from poverty of de mind. And we go have a good time telling people bout de bloodthirsty village a Mayaro, an de fools dat live here. Come boy.

KEN: Boy, I en no boy, but I go come wit you like Robinson Crusoe an he Friday, an you go cook me food an buy me rum, because a could beat you in any fight from now. Go on you. (*Pushes* MAC)

MAC: Doh push me, man.

KEN: Go, a tell yer. (*Pushes him*)

(MAC *walks out.*)

MAC: Well look at my crosses, me mind gone again.

(MAC *goes.*)

KEN: A said greeting wen a come in an a say greetings wen a go out, because a tank all yer, all a all yer, fer turning me into a real saga boy an Bad John. From now on I go romance an fight wit de best an all a meet, till wat de almond tree didn't do, de good Lord go do, an in he good time. (KEN *goes out.*)

MIKEY: *(Picking up tables)* So after all dat? Yer mean all we left wit is peace? Peace, ter drink? Le we fire one, girl.

(PEGGY goes to get bottle, glass. STANLEY goes to her at bar.)

STANLEY: Am. Peggy soon as a run home an change, de post mistress could marry we. Wha yer say?

(PEGGY turns her back on him.)

PEGGY: Oh Lord, oh Lord, oh Lord. A lose 'im, a lose 'im, a lose de only Playboy a de West Indies. *(Goes into room)*

END